TOP **10**
HONG KONG

LIAM FITZPATRICK,
JASON GAGLIARDI AND
ANDREW STONE

EY

D0892831

H46 640 944 X

Left **Star Ferry** Centre **Bird Garden** Right **View from the Peak**

DK

LONDON, NEW YORK,
MELBOURNE, MUNICH AND DELHI
www.dk.com

Produced by Blue Island Publishing, London

Printed and bound in Malaysia by
Vivar Printing Sdn.Bhd

First published in the UK in 2002 by
Dorling Kindersley Limited
80 Strand, London WC2R 0RL

A Penguin Company

13 14 15 16 10 9 8 7 6 5 4 3 2 1

Copyright 2002, 2013 © Dorling Kindersley
Limited, London

Reprinted with revisions 2005, 2006,
2009, 2011, 2013

A CIP catalogue record is available from
the British Library.

ISBN 978 1 4093 7340 7

Within each Top 10 list in this book,
no hierarchy of quality or popularity is
implied. All 10 are, in the editor's
opinion, of roughly equal merit.

MIX
Paper from
responsible sources
FSC™ C018179

Contents

Hong Kong's Top 10

The information in this DK Eyewitness Top 10 Travel Guide is checked regularly.
Every effort has been made to ensure that this book is as up-to-date as possible at the time of going to press. Some details, however, such as telephone numbers, opening hours, prices, gallery hanging arrangements and travel information are liable to change. The publishers cannot accept responsibility for any consequences arising from the use of this book, nor for any material on third party websites, and cannot guarantee that any website address in this book will be a suitable source of travel information. We value the views and suggestions of our readers very highly. Please write to: Publisher, DK Eyewitness Travel Guides, Dorling Kindersley, 80 Strand, London, WC2R 0RL, UK, or email: travelguides@dk.com.

Cover: Front – **Dorling Kindersley**: Chris Stowers bl; **SuperStock**: Steve Vidler main image. Back – **DK Images**: tr; Nigel Hicks tl; Chris Stowers tc. Spine – **DK Images**: Chris Stowers b. Front Flap – **Dorling Kindersley**: Chris Stowers br.

Left **Ten Thousand Buddhas Temple** Centre **Lantau** Right **Window of the World, Shenzhen**

Left **Hong Kong skyline** Right **Temple guardian deity**

Following pages **Central district at night**

HONG KONG'S TOP 10

HONG KONG'S TOP 10

⛣ Hong Kong's Highlights

"A dream of Manhattan, arising from the South China Sea." For succinctness, modern travel writer Pico Iyer's description of Hong Kong has yet to be bettered. From opium port to Cold War enclave to frenetic financial capital, Hong Kong has never been boring. This is the hedonistic engine room of cultural fusion: East meets West in high style, and the results astonish and delight. Prepare to experience one of the most dramatic urban environments ever conceived.

The Peak
Take the tram to the lofty heights of Victoria Peak for an amazing view of the city (see pp8–9).

Statue Square
Hong Kong Island's northeast is the region's administrative centre. Colonial remnants and exciting modern architecture stand next to each other around Statue Square (see pp10–11).

Mai Po Marsh
Mai Po
Yuen Long
Sha Po Tsuen
Kam Tin
Pat Heung
Lam Tei
Yuen Kong
Shek Kong
NEW
Yueng Siu Hang
Tai Lam Country Park
Tin Fu Tsai
Tuen Mun
Sham Tseng
Tsuen Wan
Tsing Shan Wan (Castle Peak Bay)
Tsing
Shek Wan
Chek Lap Kok
Discovery Bay
Tung Chung
Lantau Island
Mui Wo
10 Lantau Peak
Cheung Sha
Chimawan Peninsula
Shek Pik
9 Cheung Chau Island
West Lamma Channel

5 ⌐————— miles ¬0 ⌐ km —————⌐ 5

Happy Valley Races
Horseracing below the high-rises: Happy Valley is where Hong Kongers go to play (see pp12–13).

Star Ferry
Ignore the subterranean road and rail links between Hong Kong Island and Kowloon. The thrilling way to cross the water is on the Star Ferry (see pp14–15).

Stanley

An old fort steeped in colonial history and reminders of World War II, Stanley on the Southside of Hong Kong Island is a peaceful diversion from the frenetic city *(see pp16–17)*.

Temple Street Night Market 6

Kowloon is at its most atmospheric at night. Head up the peninsula to the narrow lanes of Yau Ma Tei for some serious haggling *(see pp18–19)*.

Heritage Museum 7

Near Sha Tin in the New Territories, Hong Kong's best museum is a must. Splendid high-tech audio-visual displays cover the region's rich cultural heritage and natural history *(see pp20–21)*.

[Map of Hong Kong region with labelled places: Sheung Shui, Fanling, Pat Sin Leng Country Park, Plover Cove Country Park, Ting Kok, Shuen Wan, Tai Po, Tan Chung, Tai Po Kau, Tolo Harbour, Wu Kai Sha, Ma Liu Shui, Shek Hang, Sai Kung Country Park, Sharp Peak, Tai Long Sai Wan, ng Mun try Park, Fo Tan, Ma On Shan Country Park, Siu Lek Yuen, Sha Tin, Tai Mong Tsai, Sai Kung, Sheung Kwai Chung, Pak Tin, Lion Rock Country Park, Wo Mei, Kowloon Tong, KOWLOON, Tseng Lan Shue, Mong Kok, Kowloon City, Tai Po Tsai, Hung Hom, Lam Tin, Tsim Sha Tsui, Yau Tong, Tai Wan Tau, Wan Chai, Quarry Bay, Central, Shau Kei Wan, Hong Kong Island, Aberdeen, HONG KONG, Stanley, Hok Tsui Shan, South China Sea, rdeen, mma land. Numbered markers 1–8 placed on map.]

Tai Long Wan Coastline 8

The remote, rugged Sai Kung Peninsula in the New Territories is the place to find Hong Kong's finest beaches *(see pp22–3)*.

Cheung Chau Island 9

Of the many islands around Hong Kong, tiny Cheung Chau is arguably the loveliest, with traces of old China *(see pp24–5)*.

Big Buddha and Po Lin Monastery 10

In the middle of hilly Lantau Island, Po Lin Monastery is a major destination for devotees and tourists alike. The extraordinary seated Big Buddha image facing the monastery can be seen from miles away *(see pp28–9)*.

TOP 10 The Peak

With Hong Kong's most spectacular views, cooler climes and quiet wooded walks, it's no wonder Victoria Peak is so popular with tourists and the super rich who occupy the exclusive properties clinging to its high slopes. The Peak Tram takes under 10 minutes to reach Victoria Gap, pinning you to your seat as it's hauled up the sheer slope at the end of a single cable (don't worry, its safety record is spotless).

Terrace dining

The Peak Tram

🔗 If the weather is misty or there's low cloud, put off a visit to the Peak until a clearer day as the chances are you'll be able to see very little.

🔗 In the Peak Tower, Café Deco's smart interior, wide food choices and good service make it an excellent drinking and dining stop. For fantastic sea views over to Lamma Island dine or drink in the Peak Lookout's lovely garden terrace.

• Map E5 • Peak Tram 7am–midnight daily
• Single/return HK$28/$40 • Bus 15C from Central Star Ferry
• 2522 0922
• www.thepeak.com.hk

Top 10 Sights

1. Peak Tower
2. Galleria
3. The Peak Lookout
4. Barker and Plantation Roads
5. Pok Fu Lam Country Park
6. World's Most Expensive House
7. Victoria Peak Garden
8. Old Peak Rd
9. View near Summit
10. Lugard and Harlech Roads

Peak Tower
The Peak Tram empties into an anvil-shaped mall *(below)*, containing shops, restaurants and the Sky Terrace viewing gallery. Standing at 428 m (1,404 ft), this is the highest viewing platform in a city full of vertiginous observation points. The commercial emphasis may grate, but children will enjoy Madame Tussaud's waxworks.

Galleria
Although the imposing Peak Tower mall is hardly sensitive to its grand setting there is a good range of places to eat and drink inside its Galleria, with great views down onto city and harbour, and across to Lamma Island.

The Peak Lookout
This much-loved, upmarket drinking and dining favourite boasts a lovely garden terrace, great food, an excellent wine list and a friendly ambience.

4 Barker and Plantation Roads

These usually quiet (although pavement-free) roads are worth wandering for a peep at some of the Peak's pricier properties, including 23 Severn Road (No. 6 below). Most have amazing harbour views. But dream on. You would have to be a millionaire just to afford a two-bedroom flat here.

5 Pok Fu Lam Country Park

For a gentle half-hour ramble, head down Pok Fu Lam Reservoir Road, then catch a bus back into town.

6 World's Most Expensive House

In 1997 an offer of HK$900m for the property at 23 Severn Road was, incredibly, refused. Weeks later, prices crashed, and by 2001 the house was valued at a "mere" third of the price.

7 Victoria Peak Garden

The steep struggle up Mount Austin Road or the longer route along the Governor's Walk to these well-tended gardens (right) is worth the effort. The viewing platform faces Lamma Island.

8 Old Peak Rd

This former footpath up the Peak before the Peak Tram arrived is pleasant and shaded. Surfaced, but incredibly steep, it is best saved for a descent – detour onto Tregunter Path near the bottom to avoid the traffic.

9 View near Summit

The summit itself is fenced off and covered by telecom masts, but the views from the edges of Victoria Peak Garden are excellent (above).

10 Lugard and Harlech Roads

The effortless way to see most of the best views on offer from the Peak is on the shaded, well-paved, 2-mile (3-km) circular walk along Lugard Road and Harlech Road. It also makes a terrific jogging track with a view.

The Peak Tram

Despite the fact that a single steel cable hauls the tram up a long and incredibly steep track, the Peak Tram has a faultless safety record since the service opened in 1888. The most severe disruption to services came in the 1960s when torrents of water from an especially violent storm washed part of the track away.

⑩ Central's Statue Square

Stand in Central district's Statue Square and you're right in the region's financial, political, historical and social heart. Among the steel and glass of sleek skyscrapers surrounding the square are a few colonial remnants, including the handsome Neo-Classical Legislation Council Building where Hong Kong's usually low-key political demonstrations take place. Shopping, a much more popular Hong Kong pursuit than politics, goes on inside the swanky boutiques opposite.

Thomas Jackson statue

Top 10 Sights

1. Bank of China Tower
2. Shopping Malls
3. The Cenotaph
4. Chater Garden
5. Court of Final Appeal
6. The Legislative Council Building
7. Mandarin Oriental
8. Thomas Jackson Statue
9. HSBC Bank Headquarters
10. Sunday Filipino Fiesta

Bank of China Tower

🌀 For a terrific bird's-eye view over Central and the harbour, head to the viewing gallery on the 43rd floor of the Bank of China Tower. Alternatively, try the wraparound terrace at Sevva Bar and Restaurant *(see p64)*.

🔵 If you fancy picnicking in the square or in nearby Chater Garden, try the fantastic pastries, cakes and quiches from the Mandarin Oriental's Cake Shop, which is at the edge of the square.

• Map L5

① Bank of China Tower

Looming over the HSBC building is the imposing 70-storey Bank of China Tower. It was designed by the renowned architect I M Pei. The tower is a dizzying 368 m (1,207 ft) high. It doesn't please everyone – those who know about feng shui say it projects negative vibes onto other buildings.

② Shopping Malls

Two of Hong Kong's most upmarket and, of course, pricey shopping malls – the busy Landmark Centre and the less busy Prince's Building *(see p63)* – sit next to Statue Square. Within these hallowed temples to conspicuous overspending are many of the city's most exclusive and elegant boutiques, including the likes of Armani, Gucci and Prada.

③ The Cenotaph

Standing at the northern edge of Statue Square, the Cenotaph *(left)* is a memorial to those who died in the two World Wars.

For more about Hong Kong's modern buildings See pp42–3

Chater Garden

Despite the prime real-estate value on the site of what used to be the old pitch of the Hong Kong Cricket Club, the small but well-tended Chater Garden *(below)* sprang up instead of a skyscraper. It's free to enter and makes a good place to enjoy a cold drink and rest tired legs.

Court of Final Appeal

Behind the HSBC building, a handsome mid-19th-century redbrick building used to house a French Catholic mission and the old colony's first Government House. Today it serves as a court of law.

HSBC Bank Headquarters

On its completion in 1985, Sir Norman Foster's bold building was the most expensive ever built, costing more than HK$5bn. The edifice is said to have the strongest feng shui in Hong Kong. Rubbing the paws of the bank's handsome lions *(above)* is said to bring good luck.

Sunday Filipino Fiesta

Hundreds of young Filipinos and Indonesians, mostly domestic workers enjoying their only day off, occupy almost every spare bit of public space in Central.

The Legislative Council Building

One of Hong Kong's last remaining colonial buildings, the elegant Neo-Classical Legislative Council building *(right)*, which used to house the Supreme Court, now serves as Hong Kong's parliament.

Suffocating Suffrage

During Handover negotiations *(see p31)*, China was adamant that Hong Kong's Legislative Council would be as democratic under Chinese rule as under the British (in other words, it could be argued, hardly at all). When Chris Patten, the last governor, tried introducing greater representation, China dubbed Patten, among other things, "a strutting prostitute" and "serpent".

Mandarin Oriental

It's hard to believe, but the Mandarin Oriental was once Hong Kong's tallest building. Today its graceful exterior seems overwhelmed by the ceaseless traffic, but inside it's still one of Hong Kong's finest hotels.

Thomas Jackson Statue

Appropriately enough, one of Hong Kong's few remaining statues, of a 19th-century banker, is in Statue Square. The Japanese army removed one of Queen Victoria, which gave the square its name.

🔟 Happy Valley Races

Feel the earth move beneath thundering hooves as you cheer the finishers home in the ultimate Hong Kong night out. Races have been held at Happy Valley – the widest stretch of flat land on Hong Kong Island, originally a swamp – since 1846. Today the action takes place beneath twinkling high-rises making for one of the most atmospheric horseracing tracks in the world.

A winner

Pre-race parade

🕐 If you don't want to spend the whole evening at the races, arrive after the first few races have been run, when admission is free.

🍴 Moon Koon Restaurant (2966 7111), on the second floor of the main stand, offers good, reasonably priced Chinese food. Advance booking is required on race nights.

• Less than a mile (1 km) south of Causeway Bay on Hong Kong Island
• Map P6
• Meets Wed, Sat & Sun (Sep–Jul) • Dial 1817 for race details • www.hkjc.com • www.happyvalleyracecourse.com
• Adm HK$10
• Racing Museum 2966 8065; 10am–5pm Tue–Sun; free
• Come Horseracing Tour 2316 2151, call ahead for prices

Top 10 Sights

1. Wednesday Night Races
2. The Big Screen
3. Racing Museum
4. View from Moon Koon
5. Come Horseracing Tour
6. Silver Lining Skeleton
7. The Crowd
8. Types of Bet
9. Where to Bet
10. Jockey Club Booths

Wednesday Night Races

The most exciting scheduled races are fortnightly on Wednesday evenings. For the full atmosphere, jump on a Happy Valley-bound tram and bone up on the form in the Wednesday *Racing Post* on the way. The first race is usually at 7:30pm.

The Big Screen

The huge screen facing the stand *(below)* carries all the statistics racegoers need from the results of the last race to odds on the upcoming one. There are also live race pictures or replays, ensuring no one misses any of the action on the ground.

Racing Museum

The small and neat museum at Happy Valley details Hong Kong's racing history along with a selection of Chinese art celebrating the horse. Learn the story of the old trade in prized Mongolian and Chinese ponies. Don't aim to combine it with an evening at the races, however. It is closed during meetings.

View from Moon Koon

For a fantastic track-side view while you eat, head to the Moon Koon Restaurant. Racing and dining packages are available.

The Crowd

Happy Valley has a 55,000 capacity but is so popular that it sometimes sells out before the day. The enthusiasm among the big-betting, chain-smoking punters is infectious. Stand in the open next to the track where you'll get the full effect of the roar from the stands and a good view of the finishing line.

Where to Bet

Bets are placed at the counters at the back of each floor of the main stand. Pick up the right betting slips next to the counters, fill them in and take them to the counter with your stake money. If you win, wait for a few minutes after the race, then go to the same counter to collect your winnings.

Jockey Club Booths

For help and advice on placing bets go to the friendly, helpful Jockey Club officials at the booths between the main entrance and the racetrack. The Jockey Club is the only organization allowed to take bets in Hong Kong. The tax it collects makes up a small but significant percentage of government revenue, but is being threatened by illegal and online betting. Jockey Club profits go to local charities.

Come Horse-racing Tour

Splendid Tours and Grey Line both run the Come Horseracing Tour during scheduled race meetings on Wednesdays, Saturdays and Sundays. Tours include entry to the Members' Enclosure, welcome drink, buffet meal and guide service.

Silver Lining Skeleton

Silver Lining, Hong Kong's most famous horse, was the first to win more than HK$1m. The equine skeleton takes pride of place in a glass cabinet at the Racing Museum.

Types of Bet

Different ways to bet include simply guessing the winner; a place (betting your horse comes 1st or 2nd, or 1st, 2nd or 3rd if seven or more horses race); a quinella (picking 1st and 2nd in any order); and a quinella place (predicting any two of the first three horses in any order).

Hong Kong's biggest payout

A then world record total of US$92m was paid out at Happy Valley's sister track, Sha Tin, in 1997. Over 350 bets of HK$1.30 each collected HK$260,000.

⊤⁰₁₀ Star Ferry

One of Hong Kong's best-loved institutions, the Star Ferries have plied between Kowloon and Hong Kong Island since 1888. They are still used by commuters despite the advent of rail and road tunnels beneath the harbour. A ferry ride offers a thrilling perspective on the towering skyscrapers and the jungle-clad hills of Hong Kong Island. Take an evening voyage for the harbour's neon spectacle, The Symphony of Lights, when 45 harbour buildings put on a light and sound show.

Batwing junk

Crewmen, Star Ferry

✪ The HKTB office in the Tsim Sha Tsui Star ferry building is the most convenient place to pick up brochures, get help and advice, and to buy Star Ferry models and other souvenirs.

☕ The Pacific Coffee Company inside the terminal serves a reasonable cup of coffee. Alternatively try the fresh lemonade and free cookie samples from Mrs Fields.

• Map L4 • Ferries 6:30am–11:30pm daily. Frequency varies from 6 to 12 minutes • Ferry tours of the harbour also available • www. starferry.com.hk • 2367 7065
• Symphony of Lights every night at 8pm
• www.tourism.gov.hk/ symphony

Top 10 Sights

1. The Fleet
2. Clocktower
3. Star Ferry Crew
4. Star Ferry Routes
5. Skyline South
6. Victoria Harbour
7. Sightseeing Bargain
8. Ferry Decks
9. Ocean Terminal
10. Skyline North

The Fleet
In the early days, four coal-fired boats went back and forth between Hong Kong and Kowloon. Today 12 diesel-powered vessels operate, each named after a particular star (with the night-time glare and pollution, they may be the only stars you're likely to see from the harbour).

Star Ferry Crew
Many Star Ferry crew members still sport old-fashioned sailor-style uniforms, making popular subjects for camera-toting visitors. Watch out, too, for the pier crewmen catching the mooring rope with a long billhook.

Clocktower
Standing next to the Tsim Sha Tsui Star Ferry, the landmark clocktower is the last remnant of the old Kowloon railway terminus. This was the poetic final stop for trains from the mainland, including the Orient Express from London. The terminus has since moved east to prosaic Hung Hom.

Star Ferry Routes
The ferries operate between Tsim Sha Tsui and Central, and Tsim Sha Tsui and Wanchai. They run every 8 to 20 minutes depending on the time of day.

Victoria Harbour
Victoria harbour is the busiest stretch of water in Hong Kong, teeming with activity. Keep your eyes peeled at the weekend for the last remaining bat-wing sailing junk to be found in this part of China.

Ferry Decks
The lower and upper decks used to be first (upper) and second (lower) class compartments. Today the extra cents buy access to the air-conditioning section during the hottest months, and afford a better view of the city and refuge from sea spray on choppy days.

Ocean Terminal
Just north of the Tsim Sha Tsui terminal, Hong Kong's cruise ships dock, including the world's most famous liners. Some US warships also dock here during port calls.

Skyline North
As you approach Kowloon with Hong Kong Island behind you, you'll see the Arts and Cultural Centre, closest to the shore. Behind it rises the grand extension of the Peninsula Hotel, with the huge ICC tower gleaming to the west. The New Territories' craggy hills loom in the background.

Skyline South
As you cross Victoria Harbour, on the far left are the glass and flowing lines of the Convention Centre (right) in Wanchai and above it the 373-m (1,223-ft) tower of Central Plaza. Further left are the Bank of China's striking zig-zags, and the struts and spars of the HSBC building. However, the real giant is Two International Finance Centre (see pp42–3), Hong Kong Island's tallest skyscraper at a colossal 420 m (1,378 ft).

Sightseeing Bargain
With fares ranging from just HK$2.40 to HK$3, the Star Ferry is one of Hong Kong's best sightseeing bargains.

For more ways to get around Hong Kong **See p138**

Stanley

Originally a sleepy fishing haven, Stanley was the largest settlement on Hong Kong Island before the British moved in. The modern town, hugging the southern coast, still makes a peaceful, pleasant escape from the bustle of the city. Traffic is minimal, and the pace of life relaxed, with plenty of excellent places to eat, good beaches and a large market to search for clothes, silks and souvenirs. Stanley is also the place to glimpse colonial Hong Kong and an older Chinese tradition seen at the Tin Hau Temple.

Stanley market

Murray House

⚙ If you hate crowds, avoid Stanley at weekends when the town and market become very busy and the buses to and from Central fill up.

Sit at the front of the top deck of the bus to fully appreciate the dramatic coast road out to Stanley.

🍴 For alfresco dining, The Boathouse on Stanley's waterfront offers a British pub-style menu and decent sea views (see p77).

• Map F6 • Buses 6, 6A, 6X, 66 or 260 from Central • Stanley market 9am–6pm daily • www. hk-stanley-market.com

Top 10 Sights

1. Market
2. Murray House
3. Old Police Station
4. Waterfront
5. Stanley Beach
6. Tin Hau Temple
7. War Cemetery
8. Stanley Fort
9. St Stephen's Beach
10. Pubs and Restaurants

Market
Reasonably priced clothes, shoes and accessories as well as plenty of tourist tat are to be found among Stanley's pleasant, ramshackle market stalls. Although it's not the cheapest or best market in Hong Kong, you may as well potter among the hundred or so stalls before heading to a café or one of the seafront eateries.

Murray House
Shifted here from its original site in Central to make way for the Bank of China Tower (see p10), this 1843 Neo-Classical relic now houses a Maritime Museum and several restaurants (right). Adjacent Blake Pier is the departure point for remote Po Toi island (see p114).

Old Police Station
The handsome building was built in 1859 and is Hong Kong's oldest surviving police station building. The Japanese used it as a head-quarters during World War II. Today it houses a restaurant.

Waterfront
The pretty waterfront makes a pleasant promenade between the market area and Murray House. The harbour was once home to a busy fleet of junks and fishing boats, but is now empty.

Stanley Beach
This fine stretch of sand is perfect for a dip and a paddle. It's the venue for the fiercely contested dragon boat races in June when the beach fills with competitors and revellers.

Tin Hau Temple
Lined with the grimacing statues of guards to the sea goddess Tin Hau, the gloomy interior of this temple is one of the most evocative in Hong Kong. It's also one of the oldest Tin Hau temples in the region, dating back to 1767.

War Cemetery
Most of the graves are the resting place of residents who died during World War II. Others date back to early colonial days, when many settlers, young and old, succumbed to a range of tropical illnesses.

Stanley Fort
The old British army barracks at the end of the peninsula is now occupied by the Chinese People's Liberation Army (closed to public).

St Stephen's Beach
Another good stretch of sand, St Stephen's is also the place to organize sailing and canoeing. Buy all you need from Stanley's shops and make use of the barbecue pits for an open-air lunch.

Pubs and Restaurants
One of Stanley's best attractions is its excellent range of restaurants and bars (see p77). A host of eateries, from Italian to Vietnamese, are lined along Stanley Main Road, facing the sea, many with outdoor seating. Murray House also contains good restaurants.

The War Dead
After Japan overran Hong Kong in 1941 (see p74), captured civilians suffered for three years under a regime of neglect, starvation and torture. The remains of thousands of servicemen and civilians who died here during the war are buried at Stanley cemetery.

Temple Street Night Market

Beneath the bleaching glare of a thousand naked light bulbs, tourists and locals alike pick their way among the stalls crowding the narrow lanes of Yau Ma Tei's Temple Street. The overwhelming array of cheap goods includes clothes, shoes, accessories, designer fakes, copy CDs, bric-a-brac and a generous helping of junk. Prices here may be a bit higher than in Shenzhen, just over the Chinese border or in some of Hong Kong's less well-known markets, but Temple Street is unbeatable for atmosphere.

Silk jacket

Browsing shoppers

🔮 A good way to tackle the night market is to start at the top by taking the MTR to Yau Ma Tei (Exit C) and walk south from Portland Street. This way you'll end up closer to the restaurants, hotels and bars of Tsim Sha Tsui when you've finished shopping.

🍜 Snack at the *dai pai dongs* (street stalls).

• Map M1–2 • The market opens at 4pm but really gets going after 7pm and goes on until as late as midnight

Top 10 Sights

1. Fortune Tellers
2. Canto Opera Street Performers
3. Dai Pai Dong
4. Reclamation St Canteens
5. Best Watches
6. Best Clothes
7. Best Leather Goods
8. Best Shoes
9. Best Accessories
10. Best Knick-knacks

1 Fortune Tellers

A dozen fortune tellers operate around the junction of Temple and Market streets. Most are face and palm readers. The caged white finches are trained to pick a fortune card from the pack in return for some seeds.

2 Canto Opera Street Performers

On some evenings musicians and singers perform popular Cantonese Opera numbers next door to the fortune tellers.

3 Dai Pai Dong

Tighter health regulations have made *dai pai dong* food stalls a rare sight, but they are alive and well at Temple Street, selling a variety of Chinese snacks, savoury pancakes, fishballs, seafood kebabs and unspecified meat offerings.

For more markets See pp38–9

Reclamation St Canteens

If you haven't had your fill from the *dai pai dong*, try the cheap noodles and rice-based food at the covered stalls on Reclamation Street. Don't mind your neighbour's table manners, it's the done thing to drop or spit gristle and bone onto the table-tops here.

Best Clothes

Amid the naff and poly-fabric horrors (beware naked flames), good buys include cheap T-shirts, elaborate silks, beaded tops and cotton dresses. Have a look at the stall on the corner of Kansu St. Further down, tailored trousers can be ordered with a four-day turnaround.

Best Leather Goods

Leather is not really Temple Street's strong point. But belts are cheap, and there are plenty of leather handbags and shoulder bags, including fake Gucci, Elle and Burberry items. Some are more convincing than others.

Best Shoes

From the very cheap flip-flops to the reasonable suede or leather shoes, bargain footwear is available almost everywhere on Temple Street, although the variety is not huge and the styles not that elegant. Don't forget to check the shops behind the stalls. A few stalls sell designer fakes.

Best Watches

It's likely to be a decent timekeeper but with no guarantees. The local makes and Western fakes are usually good value for money. One stall offers genuine, secondhand watches.

Haggling

Remember, prices given are mostly starting points and the mark-ups are significant. The merchandise here is far cheaper in China, so haggle hard (but do it with a smile), and remember the vendor is making a profit whatever price you both agree on. Begin below half the asking price and you should be able to knock 50 per cent off many items, and often a good deal more.

Best Accessories

Cheap sunglasses are easy to find in the market. Embroidered and beaded handbags and shoulder bags are also worth looking out for.

Best Knick-knacks

Mao memorabilia, old posters, coins, opium pipes and jade are found on Public Square Street. Temple Street's northern extremity is rich in kitsch plastic Japanese cartoon merchandise, including Afro Ken and Pokémon.

🔟 Heritage Museum

This modern museum, on the outskirts of Sha Tin in the New Territories, is one of Hong Kong's best. Opened in 2000, the Heritage Museum has six permanent galleries covering the culture, arts and natural history of Hong Kong and the New Territories. Exciting audio-visual exhibits, a range of temporary exhibitions and a good interactive section for children make for a fun day out.

Photograph of Tai O in 1966

Museum entrance

🕗 Combine a visit to the museum with a trip to the races at Sha Tin if you can *(see p101).*

Admission to the Heritage Museum is free on Wednesdays.

🍴 There is a small café and gift shop in the lobby.

• Map E3 • 1 Man Lam Road, Sha Tin, New Territories • 2180 8188
• MTR to Kowloon Tong, then bus 80M
• MTR: Che Kung Temple, then a five-minute walk • www.heritage museum.gov.hk
• 10am–6pm Mon, Wed–Sat, 10am–7pm Sun & public hols
• Adm HK$10 (free Wed)

Top 10 Features

1. Architecture and Design
2. Orientation Theatre
3. Children's Discovery Gallery
4. Cantonese Opera Hall
5. Thematic Exhibitions
6. Chao Shao-an Gallery
7. Courtyard
8. New Territories Culture
9. New Territories History
10. TT Tsui Gallery

Architecture and Design

The Heritage Museum building is based on the traditional Chinese *si he yuan* style, built around a courtyard. The style is still visible in the walled villages of the New Territories *(see p104).*

Key

▨	Ground floor
▨	1st floor
▨	2nd floor

Children's Discovery Gallery

The brightly coloured gallery is a vibrant, fun way to introduce children to local nature and archaeology, and the history of toys. Interactive exhibits and the child-size 3-D models are very popular with young children.

Orientation Theatre

For a brief overview of the museum, visit the Orientation Theatre on the ground floor opposite the ticket office. A short film in English and Cantonese (in rotation) explains the exhibits and the main aims of the museum.

Thematic Exhibitions
Five halls on the first and second floors house temporary exhibitions focusing on subjects varying from popular culture, contemporary art and social issues in Hong Kong, to traditional Chinese art and history.

Cantonese Opera Hall
Cantonese opera is an obscure subject. However, the sumptuous costumes, intricate stage sets and snatches of song from the elaborate operas of Guangdong and Guangxi go some way to illustrating the attraction.

Chao Shao-an Gallery
The delicate ink on scroll paintings of artist and one-time Hong Kong resident Chao Shao-an are known far beyond China. There are dozens of fine examples in the gallery (left).

New Territories Culture
Large mock-ups of old maritime and village scenes (below) recreate the pre-colonial days. The growth of the new towns, such as Sha Tin, are also covered.

Courtyard
For fresh air and interesting surroundings, head to the shaded courtyard (above) in the centre of the complex.

Hong Kong's Earliest Settlers
The New Territories History hall tells the scant story of Hong Kong's original inhabitants. Bronze Age people left behind axe and arrowheads in various parts of the territory more than 4,000 years ago, along with some mysterious rock carvings. Excavations on Lamma Island have turned up artifacts from an older Stone Age civilisation, dating back about 6,000 years.

New Territories History
The rich fauna and flora of the region are exhibited along with 6000-year-old artifacts from the early days of human habitation in Hong Kong.

TT Tsui Gallery
The works of art dating from Neolithic times to the 20th century include porcelain, bronze, jade and stone artifacts, furniture, laquerware and Tibetan religious statues.

TOP 10 Tai Long Wan Coastline

Although only a few miles from urban Hong Kong, the remote, pristine beaches on the eastern edge of the rugged Sai Kung Peninsula seem like another country. There is no rail link and few roads, so you will have to make an early start, taking a bus to Sai Kung town, another bus to Pak Tam Au, then walk the hilly 4-mile (6-km) footpath to the beach. Alternatively, hire a junk. The reward for your effort will be glorious surf, delightful hidden pools and shaded cafés.

Bridge from Ham Tin village

Ham Tin beach

⏱ Buy the HKTB's *Discover Hong Kong's Nature* for detailed information.

🍴 The only eating options are beach cafés, or you can stock up for a picnic at Sai Kung town.

• Map G3 • Take the frequent 92 bus from Diamond Hill KCR terminating at Sai Kung town, then the half-hourly 94 bus (or 96R on Sun) to Pak Tam Au. Alternatively, pick up the number 7 bus in Sai Kung, which will also take you to Pak Tam Au. Allow about 90 minutes from Kowloon or Central to the start of the path, plus at least an hour each way to hike to and from the beach
• Daily junk hire from HK$5,500, see Yellow Pages for listings

Top 10 Sights

1. Beaches
2. Natural Swimming Pools
3. Beach Cafés
4. Ham Tin to Tai Long Path
5. Surf Action
6. Pleasure Junks
7. Hakka Fisherfolk
8. Campsite
9. Sharp Peak
10. Ham Tin Bridge

Beaches
There are three excellent beaches at Tai Long Wan. Tai Wan is the most remote and unspoiled; the smallest beach, Ham Tin, has a good café and camping area; Tai Long Sai Wan is the busiest.

Natural Swimming Pools
A lovely series of waterfalls and natural swimming pools *(left)* is the area's best-kept secret. Reach them from the path running alongside the small river at the northwestern end of Tai Long Sai Wan beach.

Beach Cafés
Noodles, fried rice and hot and cold drinks are available from the modest, reasonably priced cafés on Tai Long Sai Wan and the Hoi Fung café at Ham Tin.

➡ *The AFCD's website, www.afcd.gov.hk, has detailed information under "Sai Kung East"*

Ham Tin to Tai Long Path

Take the steep half-mile (1-km) path between Ham Tin and Tai Long Sai Wan for lovely views down onto Ham Tin, Tai Wan and the mountains behind.

Surf Action

Tai Wan usually has reasonably good surf. Gentle body-boarding should always be possible, and you may even be able to surf properly when storms raise bigger swells.

Campsite

The area just east of Ham Tin village is the best place for overnight campers *(right)*, with flat ground, public toilets and a stream for fresh water. There are no hotels.

Sharp Peak

The prominent 468-m (1,497-ft) summit of Sharp Peak is clearly visible from Ham Tin and Tai Wan. The arduous climb up its very steep slopes rewards with spectacular views over the peninsula.

Ham Tin Bridge

If you want to keep your feet dry, the only way onto the beach from Ham Tin village is via a rickety bridge. Marvel at the makeshift engineering from nailed-together driftwood and offcuts.

Pleasure Junks

Most privately hired junks drop anchor at Tai Long Sai Wan, and their passengers head to the beach in smaller craft, making this the busiest of the three beaches.

Hakka Fisherfolk

Tai Long village *(above)* may have been first settled in prehistoric times. It was a thriving Hakka fishing village until the 1950s, when most people migrated to the city or abroad. A few elderly residents remain.

The Route Out

A good route out of Tai Long Wan is the scenic path winding southwest in gentle gradients from Sai Wan village around High Island Reservoir. Once you hit the main road outside Pak Tam Chung, there's a chance of picking up a bus or taxi back into Sai Kung town – but allow 5 hours walking just in case.

Cheung Chau Island

This tiny, charming island, a half-hour ferry ride west of Hong Kong, makes a great escape from the heat and hassles of the city, except maybe at weekends when everyone else has the same idea. The sense of an older, traditional Hong Kong is pervasive among the narrow streets, tiny shops and temples of this old pirate and fishing haven. It's possible to see most of the island in a day, and there are some lovely secluded walks. The seafood is cheap and there are small but excellent stretches of beach.

Lion, Pak Tai Temple

Cheung Chau harbour

🚲 To really nip around the island, hire a bicycle from opposite the basketball courts close to Pak Tai Temple.

Cheung Chau's famous Bun Festival is held in early May, check www.hktb. com for dates.

🍴 If you've had your fill of seafood, try Morocco's (2986 9767), by the ferry pier, which serves decent Indian, Thai and Western (but not Moroccan) fare in the evenings.

• Map C6 • Daily ferries hourly or half-hourly from Outlying Islands ferry piers

Top 10 Sights

1. Pak Tai Temple
2. Harbour
3. Venerable Banyan Tree
4. Tung Wan Beach
5. "The Peak"
6. Pirates Cave
7. Windsurfing Centre
8. Boatbuilding Yard
9. Seafood Restaurants
10. Ancient Rock Carving

Pak Tai Temple

This renovated temple is dedicated to Pak Tai, Cheung Chau's patron deity who is credited with saving islanders from plague. The temple is the centre for the annual bun festival celebrations *(see p36)*, when mounds of buns are piled up to be offered to resident ghosts. The festival dates from the time of plagues in the 19th century, which were considered to be the vengeance of those killed by local pirates.

Harbour

Although Hong Kong's fishing industry has dwindled from its heyday, plenty of commercial fishing boats still operate from Cheung Chau's typhoon shelter. Cheap cycle hire is available along the waterfront.

Venerable Banyan Tree

On Tung Wan Road is a tree *(below)* that is thought to be the source of Cheung Chau's good fortune. It is so revered by islanders that in recent years a restaurant opposite was knocked down instead of the tree to make way for a road extension.

For more about Cheung Chau's bun festival See p36

Tung Wan Beach
The island's finest beach is on the east coast, 150 m (500 ft) from the west coast's ferry pier *(above)*. It is tended by lifeguards and has a shark net.

"The Peak"
A walk up the hill along Don Bosco and Peak roads will take you past some lovely old colonial houses and beautiful sea views. The cemetery on Peak Road has especially fine vistas.

Pirates Cave
The place where a 19th-century buccaneer Cheung Po-tsai supposedly stashed his booty, this "cave" is more of a hole or crevice. Take a torch to explore. The sea views nearby are lovely.

Windsurfing Centre
The family of Olympic gold-medalist Lee Lai-Shan operates the windsurfing centre and café near Tung Wan.

Boatbuilding Yard
At the harbour's northern end is a busy yard where junks are built and nets mended. Look out for the slabs of ice sliding along the overhead chute, down a mini-helter-skelter and onto the boats.

Seafood Restaurants
If you want to dine on fish or shellfish, there's plenty of choice along the seafront on She Praya Road north and south of the ferry pier. The restaurants are cheaper than other seafood centres such as Lamma. Choose from the live tanks *(above)*.

Ancient Rock Carving
In the Hong Kong region are several rock carvings in close proximity to the sea. There are some near Tung Wan beach and Cheung Chau has one facing the sea. Nothing is known of the people who carved these shapes about 3,000 years ago.

Paths and Walks
A footpath weaves around the southern edge of the island, taking in clifftop walks and a small Tin Hau Temple at the tiny Moring Beach. Heading southwest from here will take you along Peak Road past the cemetery to Sai Wan's small harbour. From here you can take a sampan shuttle back to the ferry pier at Cheung Chau village.

Following pages **The Big Buddha at Po Lin, Lantau**

TOP 10 Big Buddha and Po Lin Monastery

Once a humble house built by three monks to worship Buddha, Po Lin Monastery on Lantau Island is now a large and important temple. Its crowning glory, the giant Buddha statue facing the monastery, is an object of veneration for devotees and one of Hong Kong's most popular tourist sights. The statue dominates the area from a plinth reached by more than 260 steps. On a clear day, the view across the valleys, reservoirs and peaks of Lantau makes the climb worthwhile.

Main courtyard

View of the Big Buddha

🗝 If you can face an early start, stay overnight at the Hong Kong Bank Foundation S G Davis Hostel (2985 5610) close to the Tea Gardens and rise before dawn to see the sunrise from the summit of nearby Lantau Peak.

🍴 If you don't fancy the cheap vegetarian food available inside the temple, take a picnic and wander the nearby footpaths for a good spot.

• Map B5 • MTR to Tung Chung, then No. 23 bus, or No. 2 bus from Lantau Island's Mui Wo ferry terminal • MTR to Tung Chung, then Ngong Ping 360 Cable Car to village. Cable Car: 10am–6pm Mon–Fri, 9am–6.30pm Sat, Sun & hols; single/ return HK$86/$125
• Monastery: 9am–6pm daily; Big Buddha: 10am–6pm daily • Free

Top 10 Sights

1. The Big Buddha
2. Monastery
3. Tea Gardens
4. Ngong Ping 360 Cable Car
5. Great Hall
6. Bodhisattvas
7. Relic Inside the Buddha
8. Footpath Down to Tung Chung
9. Monks and Nuns
10. Temple Gateway

The Big Buddha
Standing a lofty 34 m (112 ft) high, this mighty bronze statue is among the largest seated Buddha images in the world. The statue, which was cast in more than 220 pieces, sits on a throne of lotus – the Buddhist symbol of purity.

Monastery
Attracted by its seclusion, Buddhist monks began arriving on Lantau in the early 20th century. The Po Lin or "precious lotus" monastery really developed as a place for pilgrimage in the 1920s when the Great Hall was built and the first abbot appointed.

Tea Gardens
The Tea Gardens just west of the Buddha statue boast their own modest tea plantation. The café sells tea leaves from the bushes and makes a pleasant shaded place to enjoy a drink or cheap Chinese meal away from the crowds.

For other sights on Lantau See pp112–17

4 Ngong Ping 360 Cable Car

The cable car ride from Tung Chung to Po Lin is an attraction in itself. The 5.7-km (4 mile), 25-minute journey provides sweeping views across the North Lantau Country Park and to the distant South China Sea (see p55).

5 Great Hall

The main temple houses three large golden Buddha images. Don't miss the ceiling paintings, the elaborate friezes around the exterior and the elegant lotus-shaped floor tiles.

6 Bodhisattvas

On each side of the staircase are statues of Buddhist saints. They are venerated for deferring heaven in order to help mortals reach enlightenment. Throw a coin into their cupped hands for luck.

7 Relic Inside the Buddha

A sacred relic of the real Buddha (a tooth in a crystal container) is enshrined within the Buddha image, but is difficult to make out. Below the statue is a display about the life of the Buddha and his path to enlightenment.

8 Footpath Down to Tung Chung

Walk back down to Tung Chung MTR via the lovely 7-km (4 mile) wooded path through the Tung Chung Valley. You will pass some small monasteries including Lo Hon, which serves cheap vegetarian lunches.

9 Monks and Nuns

You may glimpse the robed, shaven-headed nuns and monks at prayers in the old temple behind the main one. Entry is forbidden to tourists during the 3pm prayers.

10 Temple Gateway

Guarded by twin lions, the temple gateway is said to replicate the southern gate to Buddhist heaven. As found elsewhere in the temple, the gateway is decorated with reverse swastikas, which is the holy sign of Buddhism. The three Chinese characters at the top read "Po Lin Monastery".

Falun Gong at the Big Buddha

In 2000, during an official meeting on the mainland, Po Lin's abbot spoke out against the Falun Gong, the semi-religious sect that's outlawed and repressed in China. As a result, local members of the so-called "evil cult" held a big demonstration near the Big Buddha, protesting that their promotion of physical and spiritual health through tai-chi style exercises is not evil.

Left **Colonial view** Centre **Chinese refugees at border, 1950** Right **Last governor, Chris Patten**

TOP 10 Moments in History

1 4000 BC: Early Peoples
For many years, the popular version of history was that Hong Kong was a "barren rock" devoid of people when the British arrived. In fact, archaeology now shows that scattered primitive clans had settled by the seaside on Hong Kong Island and the New Territories six millennia ago. Their diet was not politically correct by today's standards: bone fragments show they liked to eat dolphin.

19th-century pirate

2 AD 1127: Local Clans
When marauding Mongols drive the Song dynasty emperor's family out of the imperial capital of Kaifeng, one princess escapes to the walled village of Kam Tin in the New Territories, where she marries into the powerful Tang clan.

3 1841: The British Take Hong Kong Island
In a decisive move during the First Opium War between China and Britain, Captain Charles Elliot of the British Royal Navy lands on Hong Kong Island and plants the Union Jack on 25 January. The 8,000-odd locals seem to take it in their stride, but China and

Britain continue to fight over other Chinese trading cities. The 1842 Treaty of Nanking cedes Hong Kong Island to Britain.

4 1860: Land Claim
The good times are rolling in Hong Kong, where the population has now swelled to more than 86,000. The island is becoming cramped, however, and after a series of further skirmishes between Britain and China, the Kowloon Peninsula and Stonecutter's Island are ceded to Britain.

5 1898: The 99-Year Lease
Britain digs in, turning Hong Kong into a mighty fort. Lyemun at the eastern end of the island bristles with guns and the world's first wire-guided torpedo. Breathing space and water supplies are assured when on 1 July, the 99-year lease of the New Territories is signed in Peking.

6 1941: Japanese Occupation
Hong Kong has guns galore defending the sea, but the Japanese

Left **Japanese soldiers captured by the British, 1945** Right **View of downtown Hong Kong, 1950s**

Chinese soldiers, morning after Handover

come by land. They have little trouble breaching the aptly named Gin Drinkers Line – a motley string of pillboxes. Hong Kong is surrendered two days before Christmas, beginning a brutal three-year occupation.

1950: Economic Miracle
The territory's economic miracle begins to unfold, as incoming refugees from China provide an eager workforce, and British rule keeps things on an even keel. Hong Kong's transformation into a manufacturing centre begins.

1997: Handover
Following the 1984 Sino-British joint Declaration, when Deng Xiaoping promised to preserve Hong Kong's autonomy under "One Country, Two Systems", Britain hands Hong Kong back to China at midnight on 30 June 1997. The ceremony appears an anticlimax after years of escalating political tensions.

1998: Financial Crisis
Asia's economic "tigers" are humbled as years of living on borrowed money finally take their toll. Hong Kong is not as badly hit as some countries, but the financial crisis bites nonetheless.

2008: Universal Suffrage
Pro-democratic groups push for a democratic political system based on Universal Suffrage to be adopted in Hong Kong, but it remains unlikely in the immediate future.

Top 10 Movers and Shakers

1 Jorge Alvares
In 1513 the Portuguese navigator Alvares becomes the first European to visit Hong Kong.

2 Cheung Po-tsai
The Lantau-based pirate king Cheung Po-Tsai wreaks havoc with international traders in 1810.

3 Lin Zexu
Commissioner Lin Zexu is appointed by China in 1839, with the task of ending the trade in imported opium.

4 Captain Charles Elliot
Flag-planter Captain Charles Elliot claims Hong Kong Island for Britain in 1841.

5 Sir Henry Pottinger
Pottinger becomes Hong Kong's first governor. He turns a blind eye to illicit shipments of opium.

6 Dr Sun Yat-sen
The reformer blasts China as "chaotic and corrupt" during a lecture at Hong Kong University in 1923. Economic boycott of the colony follows.

7 Rensuke Isogai
In 1941 the military commander begins his barbaric reign as Japan's wartime governor of Hong Kong.

8 Deng Xiaoping
The Chinese premier sticks to his principles during Handover talks in 1984.

9 Chris Patten
Lachrymose last governor Chris Patten waves goodbye to Hong Kong in 1997.

10 Tung Chee-hwa
The shipping magnate Tung Chee-hwa takes Hong Kong's helm after Handover.

Left **Traditional tonics** Centre **Junk** Right **Tai chi**

🔟 Ways to Experience the Real China

1 Spend a Night at the Opera

Operatic figures

Cantonese opera might sound discordant to the untrained ear, but make no mistake, this is a fine and ancient art. It combines song, mime, dancing, martial arts and fantastic costumes and make-up and can go on for six hours or more. Call the HKTB *(see p139)* for details of performances.

2 Ride on a Junk

We've all seen iconic images of junks, blood-red batwing sails unfurled as the sun sets over Victoria Harbour. Unfortunately, the images are all of the same boat. The beautifully restored *Duk Ling* (which means "clever duck" in Chinese) is one of the few masted sailing junks left.
⊗ *Tours depart from Central Pier 9, Hong Kong Island 2pm & 4pm Thu, 11am & noon Sat • Advance booking advisable • 2573 5282 • www.dukling. com.hk • Adm*

3 Feast on Dim Sum

Dim sum is commonly translated as "touch the heart", although in some establishments it may also touch your wallet. The small steamed snacks in bamboo baskets are delivered by grumpy old ladies with trolleys.

Dim sum

4 Visit a Market

Hong Kong's wet markets can bring on instant culture shock for those tourists who are more used to the orderly atmosphere of supermarkets. Tiptoe through rivers of blood, past gizzards and buzzing flies as hawkers yell and housewives bargain.

5 Go for a Traditional Tonic

For a taste of the real China, try a bowl of tonic tea from streetside stalls. These bitter brews are concocted from herbs according to traditional Chinese medicinal principles of whether they are "cooling" or "heating". The Lo Cha Di Yat Ka labels all its offerings in English.
⊗ *Crn Luard and Hennessy Rds, Wan Chai • Map N6*

6 Try Foot Reflexology

Vice-like hands seek out pressure points linked to vital organs. The procedure is painful, and you might be embarrassed about your feet, but you will feel so good when they stop. Reflexologists abound in Happy Valley. Try On Wo Tong. ⊗ *1/F Lai Shing Bldg, 13–19 Sing Woo Rd (and three other branches) • 2893 0199*

For 10 favourite dim sum appetizers **See p51**

Left **Chinese New Year** Right **Market produce**

Aim for Everything Zen

For a modern take on ancient China, check out the Chi Lin Nunnery in Kowloon. This gorgeous replica of a seven-hall Tang Dynasty (AD 618–907) complex took 10 years to build, using traditional techniques and materials. Bliss out listening to the nuns chanting to the Sakyamuni Buddha *(see p96)*.

Experience Unbelievable Gall

She Wong Lam in the northeast of Hong Kong Island is the best place to sup on snake wine, a traditional winter tonic. The speciality is a fiery brew containing the gallbladders of five deadly snakes. ❧ *Hillier St, Sheung Wan • Map K5 • 2543 8032*

Watch a Lion Dance

Lions are thought to ward off evil and bring luck, which explains why the opening of a new building often features a troupe of wiry youths prancing about beneath a stylised lion's head. These performances are also common around Chinese New Year *(see p36)*.

Practise Tai Chi

Turn up at the Sculpture Court in front of the Museum of Art *(see p82)* in Tsim Sha Tsui at 8am on Mondays, Wednesdays and Fridays to enjoy an hour's free instruction in this gentlest of martial arts. ❧ *Map M4*

Top 10 Ways to Pamper Yourself

Spa-ing Bout
Check into the Peninsula for a stress-busting retreat at the luxurious spa. ❧ *2920 2888*

Rubbed the Right Way
Go for a deep-tissue Chinese massage and get the blood circulating. ❧ *On Wo Tong (see Reflexology entry)*

Male Pampering
The Bliss Spa at W Hong Kong offers a range of treatments for men. ❧ *3717 2797*

In a Lather
A Shanghai-style shave at the Mandarin Oriental will leave your face feeling like a baby's bottom. ❧ *2825 4888*

Love Potion No. 9
Boost your staying power with a tonic drink from one of the many kerbside Chinese medicine shops.

Geomancing the Stone
Set your house and garden in tune with the elements with a private feng shui consultation. ❧ *Raymond Lo 2736 9568*

Pins and Needles
Loosen up with an acupuncture session. ❧ *On Wo Tong (see Reflexology entry)*

Detoxify
The 45-minute detox warming body wrap at the Spa L'Occitane is divine. ❧ *2143 6288*

Put Your Feet Up
Fans rave about the traditional Shanghai pedicure at the Mandarin Oriental. ❧ *2825 4888*

The Doctor Is In
Try some alternative medicine from a traditional Chinese doctor. ❧ *Dr Troy Sing 2526 7908*

Left **Chinese fisherman** Right **Schoolgirls**

Peoples and Cultures in Hong Kong

Chinese chequers

Chinese
With a history of revolution, migration, organized crime and incessant trading, the witty and streetwise Cantonese are the New Yorkers of China, and make up the majority of Hong Kong's population. There are also large communities of Shanghainese, Hakka (Kejia) and Chiu Chow (Chaozhou) people.

British
Colonial power may have vanished, but a large British population remains, including a small but influential community of native-born. Influences are everywhere, from street names ("Lambeth Walk", "Rutland Quadrant") to school blazers.

Eurasian
The traditional role of this community of mixed European and Asian descent – as cultural and commercial brokers between East and West – remains undiminished. If anyone can claim to truly embody Hong Kong's intriguing duality, it is this young, wealthy and internationally-minded community.

Portuguese
In the Pearl River Delta since the arrival of traders in the 16th century, the Portuguese have inter-married extensively with the Cantonese. Aside from a clutch of surnames (da Silva, Sequeira, Remedios), a lasting influence has been the fostering of an addiction to egg tarts and pastries.

Indian
The history of Hong Kong's substantial Indian population (there are Hindus, Muslims and Sikhs) dates from the arrival of the British in 1841. Like the Eurasians, young Indians have rejected purely Western or Asian notions of identity, pioneering instead a synthesis of both.

Jewish
Hong Kong has one of the oldest Jewish communities in east Asia, producing patrician business dynasties (the Sassoons, the Kadoories) and one of the most colourful colonial governors (Sir Matthew Nathan, 1903–1906).

Street scene

Share your travel recommendations on traveldk.com

Indian residents, Victoria Peak

Russian
7 A few now elderly descendants are all that is left of the former émigré community. Hong Kong's White Russians were once numerous, and you still find borsch on the menu of every takeaway and coffee shop.

Overseas Chinese
8 The surging growth in British-, American- and Canadian-born Chinese (nicknamed BBCs, ABCs and CBCs respectively) has been a characteristic of the last two decades, as the well-educated children of emigrants return in search of roots and white-collar work.

Filipino
9 Most members of the largest ethnic minority stoically perform the low-paid occupations that Hong Kongers shun, working as domestic servants, drivers, waiting staff and bar room musicians, and remitting most of their income back home to the Philippines. Filipinas promenade in their thousands every Sunday at Statue Square *(see p11)*.

Australian
10 Working mostly in business and the media, the size of this community is reflected in the fact that it boasts the largest Australian Chamber of Commerce outside of Australia, and one of only two Australian International Schools in the world.

Top 10 Patois and Lingo in Hong Kong

1 Chinglish
The local patois, which freely uses sinicized English words like *sahmunjee* (sandwich), *bahsee* (bus), *lumbah* (number) and *kayleem* (cream).

2 Portuguese
Many borrowings, including *praya* (waterfront road), *joss* (a corruption of deus, or god) and *amah* (maid).

3 Anglo-Indian/Persian
Several words, including *shroff* (cashier), *nullah* (channel or watercourse) and *tiffin* (lunch).

4 Mo Lei Tau
The impenetrable slang used by young Cantonese. Based on surreal and seemingly nonsensical phrasing.

5 "Jaihng"
All-purpose slang term meaning "cool", "excellent". (As used in the Hollywood film *Wayne's World*.)

6 "Yau Mehr Liu?"
Translates roughly as "What's your talent?" but used as a streetwise greeting; a bit like "what's up?" or "*wassup?*"

7 "Godown"
Hong Kong English for warehouse or storage facility; a contraction of "go put your load down".

8 "Whiskey Tangos"
Hong Kong police slang for "white trash".

9 "Aiyah!"
The universal exclamation of disappointment, surprise or regret.

10 "Ah-"
Prefix added to names when denoting affection, as in "Ah-Timothy", "Ah-Belinda".

Left **Flowers for Chinese New Year** Centre **Bun Festival** Right **Dragon Dance, Tin Hau**

TOP 10 Festivals and Events

Fireworks, Chinese New Year

1 Chinese New Year

Hong Kong's most celebrated festival is a riot of neon and noise. Skyscrapers on both sides of the harbour are lit up to varying degrees depending on the vicissitudes of the economy, fireworks explode over the harbour, shops shut down and doormen suddenly turn nice, hoping for a handout of *lai see* (lucky money). ☜ *Three days from the first day of the first moon, usually late Jan or early Feb*

2 Spring Lantern (Yuen Siu) Festival

Also known as Chinese Valentine's Day, this festival marks the end of the traditional Lunar New Year celebrations. Canoodling couples take to the parks under the gentle glow of lanterns and peeping Tom arrests surge. ☜ *The 15th day of the lunar calendar (end Feb)*

3 Tin Hau Festival

This is the big one if you make your living from the sea. Fishermen make floral paper offerings to Tin Hau, the goddess of the sea, hoping for fine weather and full nets. (Her views on overfishing and drag-netting aren't clear.) Try the temples at Stanley, Joss House Bay or Tin Hau Temple Road. ☜ *The 23rd day of the 3rd moon (Apr)*

4 Cheung Chau Bun Festival

Talk about a bunfight. Young men used to scale 8-m (26-ft) towers covered in buns until in the 1970s they started falling off and the practice was banned. It was revived in a tamer form in 2005. ☜ *The 6th day of 4th moon (May), Cheung Chau • Map C6*

5 Ching Ming

Also known as the grave-sweeping festival, *ching ming* means "clear and bright". This is when Chinese families visit the graves of their ancestors to clear them of any weeds and wilted flowers. Many people also light incense and burn paper money. ☜ *First week of Apr*

6 Dragon Boat (Tuen Ng) Festival

Drums thunder and paddles churn the waters of Hong Kong as garish craft vie for the top prize. The

Tin Hau Festival

festival honours Qu Yuan, a 3rd-century poet-statesman who drowned himself to protest against corrupt rulers. ☜ *The 5th day of the 5th moon (early June), various venues*

Dragon boats

Hungry Ghost (Yue Laan) Festival

From the 14th day of the seventh moon, Chinese believe the gates of hell are thrown open and the undead run riot on earth for a month. Lots more "Hell money" goes up in smoke, as do various hillsides. Not a good time for hiking. ✆ *Roughly Jul, various locations*

Mid-Autumn Festival

One of the most picturesque of Hong Kong's festivals. Families brave the most appalling traffic jams to venture out into the country parks to burn candles and feast on yolk-centred mooncakes. Unfortunately, the intricate paper lanterns have increasingly been supplanted by glowing, blow-up Hello Kitty, Doraemon and Pokémon dolls. ✆ *The 15th night of the 8th moon (Aug); try Victoria Park*

Chung Yeung Festival

Put on your hiking boots. This festival commemorates a Han Dynasty scholar who took his family up a hill and came back to find the rest of his village murdered. ✆ *The 9th evening of the 9th moon (usually mid- to late Oct); visit any hilltop*

Christmas Day

Not a traditional Chinese festival, of course, but Hong Kongers have wholeheartedly embraced the more commercial aspects of Christmas. ✆ *25th Dec*

Top 10 Sporting Events

1 Asian Challenge Cup
Local football teams go head to head each Chinese New Year. ✆ *Hong Kong Stadium • 2378 3129 • Feb*

2 Rugby Sevens
The city's annual sporting event is fast rugby and beer-fuelled mayhem. ✆ *2504 8311 • www.hksevens.com • Mar*

3 Cricket Sixes
Top players take part in action around the stumps. ✆ *Kowloon Cricket Club • 2504 8102 • Oct*

4 International Dragon Boat Races
Festive boats compete on the Shing Mun River. ✆ *Sha Tin • mid-Jun*

5 International Races
Spectacular, high-profile equine competition. ✆ *Sha Tin Racecourse • Hong Kong Jockey Club 2966 8335 • www.cxhkir.com • Dec*

6 HK Badminton Open
International badminton stars on court. ✆ *Hong Kong Coliseum • 2504 8318 • Nov*

7 Standard Chartered Hong Kong Marathon
The gruelling race starts at Tsim Sha Tsui. ✆ *2577 0800 • www.hkmarathon.com • Feb*

8 Macau Grand Prix
Formula 3 action on the former Portuguese enclave. ✆ *8796 2268 (Macau); 2838 8680 (Hong Kong) • www. macau.grandprix.gov.mo • Nov*

9 Trailwalker
A gruelling walk over MacLehose Trail. ✆ *Oxfam 2520 2525 • Nov*

10 Hong Kong Open
Prestigious annual golf tournament. ✆ *Asian PGA 2621 6000 • Nov*

Left **Temple Street** Centre left **Western Market** Centre right **Bird Garden** Right **Goldfish Market**

Markets

Temple Street

This atmospheric market comes alive at night. Hundreds of stalls are jam-packed by 9pm, offering pirated goods and all manner of, well, junk. It used to be known as Men's Street, and many stalls still stock less-than-fashionable attire. Venture past the market and you'll stumble onto a lamplit coterie of fortune tellers and possibly a Chinese Opera recital. (See pp18–19.)

Western Market

The Western Market (in the northwest of Hong Kong Island) is situated in a gorgeous old Edwardian building, but the pickings are slim. Best bet is the excellent selection of antique and second-hand watches on the ground floor. Also a good range of fabric shops, although bargains are scarce. In a former life it housed a meat and vegetable market. ✆ *323 Des Voeux Rd Central, Sheung Wan • Map J4 • 10am–7pm*

Ladies Market

No designer labels – unless they're fake. What you'll find here is inexpensive women's clothing from lingerie to shoes. There's a decent selection of jeans, cheap food and knick-knacks galore. (See p90.)

Jardine's Bazaar and Jardine's Crescent

An open-air market area in the heart of Causeway Bay, one of Hong Kong's busiest shopping districts. All sorts of goodies here, from run-of-the-mill fashion shops to traditional barbers and Chinese medicine sellers. Sample a glass of fresh soy bean milk. ✆ *Jardine's Bazaar, Causeway Bay, Hong Kong Island • Map Q6 • 11am–8pm*

Cat Street

No, there are no more cats here than anywhere else in Hong Kong. Cat Street refers instead to the Chinese slang for odds and ends. This street and nearby

Left **Antique Buddha image, Cat Street** Right **Mao posters, Cat Street**

Busy Gage Street Market

Hollywood Road are chock full of antique and curio shops. This is the place for silk carpets, elegant Chinese furniture, Ming dynasty ceramic horsemen and Maoist kitsch. ◈ *Map J5*

Jade Market
As you might suppose, jade sellers abound – more than 450 of them at last count. Don't attempt to buy the top-grade stuff unless you're an expert and know what you are doing. But there are plenty of cheaper pieces to be found *(see p90)*.

Stanley Market
Full of tourists of the badge-sporting, flag-following variety, this can still be a fun place to shop. If you're not claustrophobic, join the hordes thronging the narrow lanes to gorge on tacky rubbish *(see p16)*. ◈ *Stanley Main St, Hong Kong Island • Map F6 • 10am–6pm*

Bird Garden
More than 70 stalls showcasing all manner of songbirds and (mostly legal) exotica, bounded by elegant courtyards, full of old men with white singlets rolled up to bare their bellies (one of Hong Kong's odder fashion statements). A flower market is nearby *(see p89)*. ◈ *Yuen Po Street, Mong Kok • 7am–8pm*

Goldfish Market
A popular spot for locals, as a fishtank in the right spot is thought to ward off bad luck. Hook a bargain on underwater furniture with an oriental flavour, or just admire the colourful creatures on show. ◈ *Tung Choi St, Mong Kok • 10am–6pm*

Gage Street
This market is worth a peek if you happen to be in Central but hardly worth a special visit. Lots of blood and guts, especially for early birds. Trucks disgorge fresh pink pig carcasses as squawking chickens ponder their final hours. ◈ *Map K5*

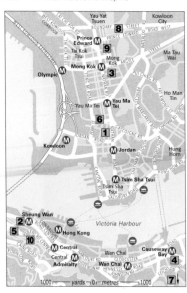

Left **Mid-Levels escalator** Centre **Taxi** Right **Open-top bus**

🔟 Transports of Delight

1 The Mid-Levels Escalator
The series of escalators in the steep Mid-Levels district of northwest Hong Kong Island is designed for commuters, but most appreciated by sightseers who can rest their legs and enjoy the fascinating sights *(opposite)*. Take a stately (and free) ascent past busy street scenes, traditional shops and apartment windows. *(See p59.)*

2 Trams
Hong Kong's trams date back to 1904, making this one of the oldest continuously used tram systems in existence. They are still one of the best ways of exploring the Hong Kong Island shoreline. Trainspotter's trivia: it's also the only double-decker tram system in the whole world.

Old-fashioned tram

3 The Peak Tram
Since 1888, this funicular railway has made the jaw-dropping ascent of Victoria Peak, and remains a must for visitors. Under the unwritten rules of colonial times, certain seats were reserved for high officials; now, seating is an amiable free-for-all. *(See p9.)*

4 Airport Express Link
Should your attention span wane on the fleeting 24-minute ride from the airport to Central, the AEL offers personal TVs in the back of every seat. Bright, shiny and a joy to use.

5 MTR
Hong Kong's underground railway is a world leader, handling three million people a day with rapid and robotic efficiency. Signs are in both English and Chinese, delays are almost unheard of, and with fares starting from the price of a cup of coffee, a trip around the city is surprisingly affordable, too.

6 Ferries
The fabulous Star Ferry *(see pp14–15)* connects Hong Kong Island to Kowloon. Pay half the price of a cup of coffee for a first-class view of one of the world's most remarkable harbours and skylines. Other ferries connect Hong Kong to the outlying islands and parts of the New Territories *(see p138)*.

For more on getting around Hong Kong **See p138**

Rickshaws

Once a common sight on Hong Kong's streets, these hand-pulled passenger wagons have gradually faded into history. For years the dwindling numbers of wizened, elderly license-holders earned a living charging tourists for photos outside Central's Star Ferry terminal. Now you will only find rickshaws in the city's museums.

Taxis

Hong Kong cabbies are as psychotic as big city cabbies everywhere. Their rudeness is legendary, but you probably would be too if you had to deal with Hong Kong traffic all day, every day. Fortunately, tighter policing means that overcharging is now a rare occurrence.

Limousines

On a per capita basis, Hong Kong probably has more Mercedes and Rolls Royces than anywhere else in the world. Some 15 of the latter are owned by the Peninsula Hotel alone – including a Phantom II dating from 1934.

Buses

Hong Kong's double-decker buses are a British legacy, although these mostly come air-conditioned and (in a universally loathed development) with onboard TVs blaring ceaseless advertising. The low cost of using them may help you overcome this irritant.

Star ferries

Top 10 Sights from the Mid-Levels Escalator

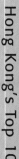

Escalator Itself
The world's longest covered escalator system is a sight unto itself.

Commuters
Some 211,000 people ride the system daily, bypassing the Mid-Levels' notorious traffic snarls.

Gage Street Market
Gaze down on this lively Chinese produce market *(see p39)*.

BoHo
("Below Hollywood Road") The start of the journey takes you through the heart of this hip quarter.

SoHo
("South of Hollywood Road"). Alight at the first stop and walk a block uphill for trendy bars and eateries *(see p60)*.

Hollywood Road
Home to antique shops, galleries, nightclubs, bars and the historic Man Mo Temple *(see p61)*.

Galleries
Several en route, many specializing in the bright new wave of Chinese art.

Rednaxela Terrace
So named because a 19th-century signwriter wrote "Alexander" from right to left, in the Chinese manner. Uncorrected to this day.

Jamia Masjid
Also known as the Shelly Street Mosque, built in 1915. One of three mosques catering to 70,000 Muslims.

Conduit Road
Where SoHo peters out, and the Mid-Levels begins amid forests of upscale apartment blocks.

Hong Kong's Top 10

Left **Bank of China, Cheung Kong Centre and HSBC** Right **HK Convention and Exhibition Centre**

Modern Buildings

HSBC interior

HSBC Building

Sir Norman Foster's striking, Bladerunner-esque edifice cost a whopping HK$5.2bn, making it the world's priciest pile when it opened in 1985. The headquarters of the Hong Kong and Shanghai Banking Corporation are reputed to have some of the best feng shui around – the building sits on a rare confluence of five "dragon lines" and enjoys unimpeded harbour views. The soaring atrium feels like a cathedral, which might explain why on Sundays the ground level is taken over by chattering Filipina maids. ◉ *1 Queen's Rd, Central • Map L5*

Bank of China

This one is also famous in feng shui circles, but more for dishing it out than possessing it – the glass-skinned tower shoots bad vibes at the old Government House and other colonial entities. Its knife-like edges were the inspiration of American-Chinese master architect I M Pei. The 70-storey, 368-m (1,207-ft) stack of prisms opened in 1990. Its viewing platform is the natural place to go for a sweeping city perspective. ◉ *1 Garden Rd, Central • Map L6 • 43/F viewing platform 9am–6pm Mon–Fri, 9am–1pm Sat*

Tsing Ma Bridge

The suspension bridge stretches from Tsing Yi Island to Lantau, a mile and a half (2.2 km) long. A striking sight, especially when lit up at night, the bridge carries the road and rail links to Chek Lap Kok airport. It opened in May 1997, having taken five years to build at a cost of HK$7.14bn. Take the MTR to Tsing Yi or catch an airport bus (but not the airport train) to view it. There's also a viewing platform at Ting Kau (*see p116*). ◉ *Map D4*

Bank of China

Two IFC Tower

The Two International Finance Centre Tower soars above Victoria Harbour. At 420 m (1,378 ft), it was Hong

Kong's tallest building until overtaken in 2010 by the International Commerce Centre. There is a large, upmarket shopping mall at its base. ✪ *Exchange Square, Central • Map L5*

Hong Kong International Airport

Sir Norman Foster strikes again. His glass-dominated passenger terminal, which opened in July 1998, is impressive. The airport is built on the specially flattened island of Chek Lap Kok. ✪ *Map B4*

Lippo Towers

These knobbly megaliths look like they have koalas clinging to the sides – a reflection of the original antipodean owner, jailbird Alan Bond. ✪ *89 Queensway, Admiralty • Map L–M6*

International Commerce Centre

At 490 m (1,600 ft) in height and with 118 storeys, this is Hong Kong's tallest building. It houses the world's highest hotel, the Ritz-Carlton, Hong Kong *(see p148)* and the sky100 Observation Deck. ✪ *1 Austin Rd West, Kowloon • Map L2*

Cheung Kong Centre

Big, boxy and glassy, the top floor is the home of business

Lippo Towers

magnate Li Ka-shing. Note how it's built perfectly parallel to the adjoining Bank of China for optimal feng shui. ✪ *Map L6*

Central Plaza

Confusingly, this is in Wan Chai, not Central. The building has 78 storeys, two fewer than The Centre, but at 374 m (1,227 ft), it's taller. Central Plaza is also the world's tallest reinforced concrete building. ✪ *18 Harbour Rd, Wan Chai • Map N5*

HK Convention and Exhibition Centre

Site of the official Handover ceremony in 1997, the Centre sprawls over a huge area over the harbour and was designed to resemble a bird in flight. ✪ *1 Expo Drive, Wan Chai • Map N5*

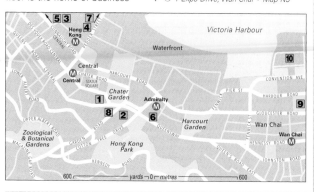

Left **Sai Kung peninsula** Centre **Birdlife, Mai Po Marshes** Right **Ma On Shan**

🔟 Areas of Natural Beauty

1 Cape D'Aguilar

It may be only 7 miles (11 km) directly south of Hong Kong's busy Central district, but Cape D'Aguilar feels like another world. The wild coastline has wave-lashed rock formations and a marine life so rich that researchers have discovered 20 species "new to science" in these waters. ❧ Map F6

Paddy fields, Sha Lo Tung

2 Hoi Ha Wan

The long inlets and sheltered coves of this 260 hectare marine park in northern Sai Kung are made for snorkelling. Stony coral and reef fish galore. ❧ Map G2

3 Mai Po Marsh

Declared a Ramsar site (that is, a wetland of international importance) in 1995, Mai Po is one of China's most important bird sanctuaries, with hundreds of resident and migratory species recorded, including many endangered ones. Other wildlife includes otters, civet cats, bats and numerous amphibians. ❧ Map D2

4 Bride's Pool

The pool is a popular picnic spot. Weekends are best avoided, but visit midweek and, with luck, you will have this glorious, wooded course of rockpools and cascades all to yourself. ❧ Map F2

5 Pat Sin Range

Hong Kong's countryside achieves a quiet grandeur among the empty valleys and sublime uplands of Pat Sin ("eight spirits"). Peaks range up to 639 m (2,095 ft), and the views are humbling. ❧ Map F2

Left **Bride's Pool** Centre **River valley, Pat Sin**

For more on Hong Kong's natural scenery visit www.afcd.gov.hk

Sharp Peak and Ham Tin beach, Tai Long Wan

The Dragon's Back

This undulating ridge snakes down Hong Kong Island's south-east corner, with plunging slopes, poetic sea views and (past Pottinger's Gap) deep wooded valleys and beaches. ◈ Map F5

Jacob's Ladder

Take these steep steps up the rock from Three Fathom's Cove, and enter an expanse of remote uplands and boulder-strewn paths, leading, in the north, to Mount Hallowes. There are exquisite views of the Tolo Channel. ◈ Map G3

Sha Lo Tung

This hidden valley is probably the closest Hong Kong comes to stereotypical ideas of classical Chinese landscape, with its old paddy fields, deserted villages, flowing streams and ancient woods. Magical. ◈ Map F2

Ma On Shan

The plateaus and grassy slopes of the 702-m (2,302-ft)

high Ma On Shan ("Saddle Mountain") allow wide-screen views of mountainous country, without the insidious intrusion of city skyline in the distance. The effect is truly majestic. ◈ Map F3

Tai Long Wan

On the Sai Kung Peninsula, survive the knuckle-whitening ascent of Sharp Peak (all loose rocks and narrow paths), and the land plunges down to your well-earned reward: the sparkling waves and white sand of Hong Kong's finest beach, Tai Long Wan (see pp22–3).

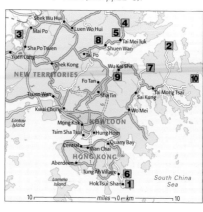

For more areas of natural beauty **See p105**

Left **Cultural Centre promenade** Centre **View from the Peak** Right **Fortune tellers, Temple Street**

Top 10 Walking Routes and Promenades

1 The Peak Circuit
Taking about an hour to complete at a gentle pace, this loop around Victoria Peak, formed by Harlech and Lugard Roads, offers jaw-dropping city panoramas to the north, boundless sea views to the south, and glimpses of millionaire homes among the greenery en route *(see pp8–9)*.

2 Temple Street Night Market
Allow plenty of time, not for the distance (Temple Street is no more than half a mile end to end), but to explore the funky pageantry of hawker stalls, fortune tellers, medicine men and opera singers that set up here every night *(see pp18–19)*.

3 The MacLehose Trail
The trail spans over 60 miles (100 km) across the New Territories, so only bona fide outdoor types will attempt the whole length. But certain sections are easily accessible (try the lovely part around the High Island Reservoir) for visitors who value the prospect of being back at the hotel bar by nightfall. ⊗ *Info from HKTB (see p139)* • *Map G3*

4 Central to Western via Hollywood Road
Central's futuristic office towers and concrete canyons give way to the low-rise charm of antique shops, galleries and bars the further west you go, ending up in Western's archetypal Chinese shopping streets and docksides. A must. *(See pp58–61.)*

5 Cultural Centre Promenade
This walkway from the Kowloon Star Ferry, around past the InterContinental, is notable for a statue of kung fu movie legend Bruce Lee. It also has great views of Hong Kong Island's towers – see these lit to music nightly at 8pm in the "Symphony of Lights" *(see pp82–3)*.

6 Nathan Road
A joyously tacky and tawdry strip, the Golden Mile, Hong Kong's own Broadway, runs up the Kowloon peninsula, passing hotels and tourist shops at the

Left **Quiet road at the Peak** Right **Temple Street Night Market**

Left **Nathan Road at night** Right **Cheung Chau**

upscale southern end, before downgrading into the sleazy karaoke lounges and low-rent storefronts of central Kowloon. Just don't buy any electronics along the way *(see p81)*.

The Hong Kong Land Loop

Almost all of Central's prestige commercial towers are in the portfolio of one company, Hong Kong Land, which has thoughtfully connected its properties with aerial walkways. The buildings include Jardine House, Mandarin Oriental, Princes Building and the Landmark Centre. Do the circuit, if only for the ethereal experience of seeing downtown Hong Kong without touching the ground. Ⓢ *Map L5*

The Praya, Cheung Chau

This island *praya* (or waterfront road) is everything the main drag of a backwater fishing town should be: a rambling tableau of fresh catches, boats tying up, market stalls and skipping kids. Look out for the splendid hand-pulled

water carts that are the island's only fire engines *(see pp24–5)*.

Surfer, Cheung Chau

The Central Green Trail

Just minutes from the banks, malls and offices of downtown, this signposted, hour-long trail from the Peak Tram terminus at Hong Kong Park opens up a lush hillside world of trees, ferns and rocks. A beautiful, shady surprise. Ⓢ *Map L6*

Victoria Park

One of the city's larger green sites, Victoria Park is best visited in the early morning, when tai chi devotees exercise. Throughout the day there are people-watching opportunities and restful walks, away from urban pressures *(see pp68–9)*.

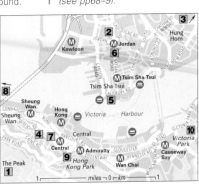

Left **Caprice** Right **Top Deck**

🔟 Restaurants

1 T'ang Court

Food at T'ang Court, the Langham Hotel's two-star Michelin restaurant, continues to astonish. Peerless creativity and insistence on *wok chi* (wok cooking at the highest achievable temperature) are the keys to T'ang Court's greatness. Ⓢ *2/F Langham Hotel, 8 Peking Road, Kowloon • Map N4 • 2132 7898 • $$$$$*

2 The Verandah

From its epic Sunday brunches, through to the speechless aplomb of its candle-lit dinners, this sleek patrician of the South-side has a stately lead over the competition. The details are sheer class (when did you last have caesar salad made, as it should be, at your tableside?) and the ambience oozes the "wow" factor *(see p77)*.

3 Gaddi's

Royalty, Hollywood stars and heads of state have dined here by the worshipful score, for in terms of French cuisine east of Suez, Gaddi's is the holy grail. Expect the big-budget works: from the aristocratic menu to stratospheric service levels. If you like it *haute*, you've found your heaven *(see p87)*.

4 8½ Otto e Mezzo Bombana

This superb contemporary Italian restaurant was upgraded from two to three Michelin stars in 2011, the first Italian restaurant outside Italy to achieve that recognition. Chef Umberto Bombana, dubbed "The King of White Truffles", weaves his culinary magic using only the freshest ingredients. The name is taken from Federico Fellini's 1963 autobiographical film *(see p65)*.

5 L'Atelier de Joël Robuchon

L'Atelier is a highly contemporary venue decorated in bright scarlet with high-top seats set around an open kitchen. The set menu options combine classic French culinary traditions with distinctive Asian

Left **The Verandah** Right **T'ang Court**

For price categories See p65

Lung King Heen

influences without ever becoming "fusion". This restaurant is simply outstanding, as its three Michelin stars imply, and is renowned especially for meat and seafood dishes *(see p65)*.

Island Tang
The 1920s period decor and Cantonese teahouse menu appear smart and simple, though ingredients such as bird's nest and abalone hint at high standards. Superior dim sum, good Peking duck and roast meats are served here, along with plenty of vegetarian options; Island Tang also boasts an impressive wine cellar with some good vintages *(see p65)*.

Lung King Heen
The world's first Chinese to earn three Michelin stars is a beautifully styled modern Cantonese restaurant. Lung King Heen means "View of the Dragon" and the inside is designed to replicate a Chinese landscape. It is particularly strong on seafood dishes and dim sum, which can be enjoyed while taking in the harbour views *(see p65)*.

Caprice
A three-star Michelin restaurant with views of the harbour, this is fine French dining at its most sumptuous; expect fine cuisine, excellent Bordeaux and Burgundy wines and lavish decor. Set-menu lunches draw a strong business crowd, while evenings and weekend lunches are definitely "see and be seen" affairs *(see p65)*.

Kung Tak Lam
Vegetarians unable to face another helping of the slop and swill that passes for much animal-free cuisine will praise the creator for Kung Tak Lam. This light and airy Shanghainese does things with vegetables that could not be done, could not even be imagined, by most vegetarian restaurants elsewhere.
○ *World Trade Center 1001, 208 Gloucester Rd, Causeway Bay • Map P5 • 2890 3127 • $$$*

Top Deck
The Jumbo floating restaurant may be a tourist trap, but the top floor has been converted into a fantastic alfresco restaurant. Top Deck is a first-class seafood venue, serving everything from tempura soft-shelled crab to tasty *bouillabaisse (see p77)*.

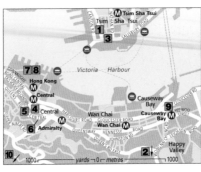

Recommend your favourite restaurant on traveldk.com

Left *Cha siu* Centre Fish drying, Cheung Chau Right Pak-choi

🔟 Hong Kong Dishes

1 Cha Siu

This is virtually Hong Kong's national dish. The name literally means "fork roast". The tender fillets of pork are roasted and glazed in honey and spices, and hung in the windows of specialist roast meat shops. *Cha siu* is classically served thinly sliced, with steamed rice and strips of vegetables.

2 Moon Cake

Made of moist pastry and various fillings, including lotus, taro, adzuki bean, whole egg yolk and occasionally coconut, the delicacy also has a quirky history: revolutionaries in imperial China used to smuggle messages to each other hidden in a moon cake's dense filling.

3 Steamed Whole Fish

In Hong Kong, fish is almost always dressed very simply, using only peanut oil, soya sauce, coriander and chives. To maximize

Steamed whole fish

freshness, restaurants keep live fish in tanks, killing and preparing them to order.

4 Hainan Chicken

Comprising chunks of steamed chicken, served slightly warm or cold, and dipped in an aromatic oil made with spring onions and ginger, this dish has become everyday comfort food. It is traditionally accompanied by a rich chicken broth, a few vegetables and rice steamed in chicken stock for flavour.

5 Brisket of Beef

Requiring up to 8 hours of slow cooking, preparation of this Hong Kong classic is an art. Households and restaurants guard their individual recipes, but all involve the classic five Chinese spices, rock sugar and tangerine peel. It's served in an earthenware pot as a main course, or as a topping for rice or noodles. Given its richness, it is particularly enjoyed in winter.

Dried meats

6 Water Spinach

The leafy, hollow-stemmed vegetable can be prepared with various seasonings, from the quotidian oyster sauce to garlic and shrimp paste. At its best when stir-fried with potent chillies and semi-fermented tofu.

7 Wontons

Done properly, this marvellous prawn and pork ravioli is poached in a

Wonton soup

stock made from shrimp roe, aniseed and other spices, and served with fresh egg noodles and soup.

8 Fish Balls

A daily food for many Hong Kongers, either on skewers as snacks or served with noodles in broth to make a meal. Traditional restaurants eschew machine production methods, and still shape these balls of minced fish, white pepper and other spices by hand, before poaching them in seafood or chicken stock.

9 Salt and Pepper Crusted Squid

You may have encountered the disastrous and greasy travesty of fried squid served up in Western Chinatowns. Banish that unpleasant memory from your mind, and prepare to discover the gloriously crisp original. Fresh squid is scored, lightly battered and flash fried with lots of salt, white pepper, chilli and garlic. The result is an addictive combination of tangy textures.

10 Lai Wong Bau

Chinese bread is shaped into buns, not loaves, and steamed rather than baked – giving it a beautifully soft and fluffy quality (no gritty whole grains here). There are many varieties of sweet bun, but *lai wong bau* is the reigning favourite, the kind of treat that children will clamour for. These buns are filled with milk, eggs, coconut and sugar. Try them piping hot on a cold winter morning.

Top 10 Dim Sum (Dumplings)

1 Har Gow
Prawns wrapped in rice flour casing – like a very plump ravioli.

2 Siu Mai
Minced pork and shrimp parcels, topped with a dab of crab roe.

3 Seen Juk Guen
Soy pastry, crisp fried with a vegetable filling. A savvy alternative to the common spring roll.

4 Gai Jaht
Chicken and ham wrapped in soya bean sheets, served in rich sauce.

5 Lohr Bahk Goh
Mashed turnip, pan-fried with chives, dried shrimp and Chinese salami.

6 Cheung Fun
Rolls of rice pastry, filled with shrimp, pork or beef, and smothered in sweet soy.

7 Chiu Chow Fun Gohr
Soft, pasty-style dumplings filled with chopped nuts, minced pork and pickled vegetables.

8 Chin Yeung Laht Jiu
Green pepper stuffed with minced fish and prawns and served in black bean sauce.

9 Ji Ma Wu
Decadent, treacle-like dessert made from sugar and mashed sesame. It is served warm from the trolley.

10 Ma Lai Goh
Wonderfully light and fluffy steamed sponge cake, made with eggs, brown sugar and walnuts.

Left **Dragon-i** Right **Kee Club**

Nightclubs

Felix

1 The shining pinnacle of Hong Kong bars is set in Kowloon's famous Peninsula Hotel. Philippe Starcke designed Felix, and the result is coolness incarnate. Let the experience envelop you, beginning with the dedicated elevators and their light effects, to the untrammelled delights of Felix's restrooms. The harbour views are an added bonus. If you plan to visit just one bar in Hong Kong, make this the one *(see p87)*.

Foreign Correspondents' Club

2 Any club that has brass plaques screwed to the bar top, commemorating members who died drinking on that spot, deserves to be a legend. Open only to members and their guests.
⊗ *2 Lower Albert Rd, Central* • *Map K6* • *2868 4092*

Di Vino

Dragon-i

3 Stunning interior design in mixed Chinese and Japanese style but with lots of New York thrown in across two completely different rooms. The Red Room dining room becomes a VIP lounge for the famous as the evening progresses, with everyone else sinking into the booths in the bronze and mirrored Playground, drinking powerful cocktails. Be stylish, or be somewhere else *(see p64)*.

Kee Club

4 An un-marked doorway on Wellington Street is the entrance to this seriously happening private club. Everyone worth knowing in Hong Kong is on its members' list, but this means that it can be hard to gain access. Inspired by the Enlightenment concept of literary and discursive salons, Kee Club can sometimes be too arty by half, but it's always worth an invitation. Assuming you're lucky enough to score one. ⊗ *6/F, 32 Wellington St, Central* • *Map K5* • *2810 9000*

Di Vino

5 This small tunnel-shaped bar crammed with beautiful people makes the perfect start to any evening. But with special prices on early evening apéritifs and around 40 wines available by the glass, it's not long before snacks become a look at the menu, a memorable Italian meal and a rather later than planned move to elsewhere *(see p65)*.

Beijing Club

6 Another glamorous member of Hong Kong's party scene is based in an old office block. Taking up three floors, this club does not believe in subtle decoration. The dance floor and main bar are on the second floor,

Left **Felix** Right **Central district at night**

a chill-out area with a massive projection screen and a balcony is on the third, and the VIP room is on the fifth floor. The regular diet of house, hip hop and R&B is spiced up with Ministry of Sound DJ events *(see p64)*.

Play

Hong Kong's largest single-floor nightclub lies in the heart of Central. It is split into three distinctive rooms, including two main rooms and a champagne bar. Top DJs and Asia's finest cocktail mixologists keep the trendy club clientele partying into the early hours of the morning. ◈ *14 Wyndham St, Central • Map K5 • 2525 1318*

Fly

Playfully designed, this smart but unstuffy club with its contemporary interior is great for a night of non-stop electronic music. The thumping Turbosound system pumps out a mix of international DJ tunes ranging from house and electric to dubstep and drum 'n' bass . ◈ *9/F 24–30 Ice House St, Central • Map K5 • 2810 9902*

Feather Boa

Away from the rowdy main strip of Staunton Street bars sits this unremarked gem, with its inconspicuous entrance, fin-de-siècle gold drapes and sofas. The crowd is young, arts- and media-slanted, and cliquey *(see p64)*.

Drop

This super-hip venue is one of the best clubs in Hong Kong. Set up by resident DJ Joel Lai, it is the place to go to dance and see Hong Kong's "beautiful people". Though small in size, it has a large bar and is extremely popular, due in part to the special club events, happy hours and top local and international DJs. It has a sister club in Shanghai. ◈ *39-43 Hollywood Rd • Map K5 • 2543 8856*

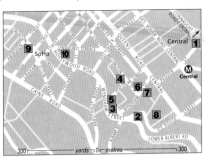

Left **Dolphin watching** Centre **Rollercoaster, Ocean Park** Right **Child, Kowloon Park**

TOP 10 Places for Children

Ocean Park

"Connecting people with nature" is what it's all about at Ocean Park. The Giant Panda Habitat, Atoll Reef, Sea Jelly Spectacular and Dolphin University exhibits will keep children engrossed for hours. Older kids will love the supervised sessions where you can touch some of the animals. The park also features nearly 30 exciting rides, including The Abyss rollercoaster and Raging River ride, plus a cable car *(see p73)*.

Ocean Park

and shrub-lined paths. Not, however, in the monkey house, where the world's largest collection of red-cheeked gibbons shriek and swing and even copulate. Also housed here are lemurs, tamarins, orangutans and 280 species of birds.

🅰 *Upper Albert Rd, Central • Map K6 • 6am–7pm daily • Free*

Science Museum

There is lots of hands-on stuff here, providing a fun and educational introduction to many facets of science. Any child with a healthy dose of curiosity will spend hours pushing buttons, pulling levers and marvelling at gadgets *(see p82)*.

Zoological and Botanical Gardens

Founded in 1864, a modicum of Victorian gentility survives here in the wrought-iron bandstand

Dolphin Watching

Be quick, because the sorry state of Hong Kong waters is killing off the rare Indo-Pacific humpback dolphins, which here in the Pearl River delta are a pale pink colour. 🅰 *Hong Kong Dolphin-watch 1528A Star House, Tsim Sha Tsui • Map B4 (dolphins) • 2984 1414 • www. hkdolphinwatch.com • Bus pick-up 9am at Kowloon Hotel TST • Wed, Fri, Sun • Adm*

Hong Kong Disneyland

The mighty mouse wisely used feng shui in the design of his latest Asian venture, but otherwise there are few nods to local culture. Adventureland, Fantasyland and Tomorrowland

Left **Mickey and Minnie Mouse at Hong Kong Disneyland** Right **Peak tram**

Left **Science Museum** Right **Old-fashioned tram**

lie beyond Main Street, USA.
◉ *Lantau Island, served by its own MTR station • 1-830-830 for hours and today's tickets • park.hongkongdisneyland.com for advance booking (recommended) • Adm*

6 Lions Nature Education Centre

The Lions Nature Education Centre is more fun than it sounds, with fruit orchards, an arboretum, rock gardens and, best of all, an insectarium. Big brothers will find plenty of interesting creepy-crawlies with which to scare little sisters.
◉ *Tsiu Hang, Sai Kung, New Territories • Map G3 • 2792 2234 • 9:30am–5pm. Closed Tue • Free*

7 Ngong Ping 360 Cable Car

The spectacular 25-minute cable car journey from the hustle and bustle of the city, across open water and up the steep hillside from Tung Chung to the Big Buddha at Po Lin, is the best funfair ride in town *(see pp28–9)*.
◉ *Lantau Island • Map B5 • 3666 0606 • www. np360.com.hk • Adm*

8 Tram Tour

Rock, rattle and roll along the front of Hong Kong Island, or take a detour around Happy Valley. Hong Kong's trams may be crowded,

slow and noisy, but they are terrific for sightseeing *(see p138)*.

9 Kowloon Park

The green lungs of Tsim Sha Tsui have a huge indoor-outdoor swimming pool, lots of gardens and great free martial arts performances on Sunday afternoons *(see p83)*.

10 Hong Kong Wetland Park

This landscaped wetlands area on the China border has bird hides, a butterfly garden, lily ponds and a mangrove circuit featuring mudskippers and fiddler crabs. There is also a great walk-through environmental display. ◉ *Tin Shui Wai, New Territories • Map C2 • 3152 2666 • www.wetlandpark.com • 10am–5pm. Closed Tue • Adm*

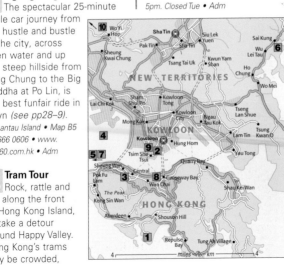

Following pages **Cheung Chau harbour**

HONG KONG'S TOP 10

Left **Red lory, Hong Kong Park** Centre **One of the escalators** Right **Central district and harbour**

Hong Kong Island – Northwest

FROM THE CORPORATE VANITIES of Central district's glass towers, through the vodka bars and galleries of SoHo, and spilling down flagstone lanes to the raucous shophouses and old docksides of Western, the Island's northwest potently concentrates all of Hong Kong's surreal contradictions. In the concrete gullies between futuristic banks and statement office blocks you'll find traditional street markets, temples and herbalists, all carrying on like some Hollywood dream of old Chinatown. These are some of the most mercantile streets in human history. A shot of snake bile wine, or a fierce macchiato? In this part of the city, you can have it all.

Sights in the Northwest

1. Hong Kong Park
2. Exchange Square and Two IFC Tower
3. Former Government House
4. The Escalator
5. SoHo
6. Sheung Wan and Western
7. Lan Kwai Fong
8. The Waterfront
9. Man Mo Temple
10. Hollywood Road

Man Mo Temple

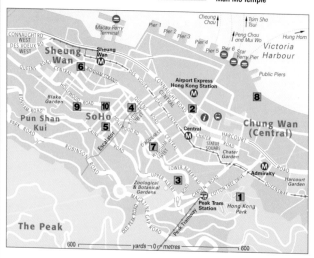

Share your travel recommendations on traveldk.com

Aviary, Hong Kong Park

Hong Kong Park

When you're tired of Central's relentless bustle, Hong Kong Park's open spaces and mature trees make an excellent escape, particularly its strikingly elegant (and free) walk-through aviary. The flowing streams and lush plant life of this improbable mini-rainforest are a peaceful and shaded home to scores of exotic bird species. The park also has lakes, a large conservatory, a viewing tower and the free Museum of Teaware, which is located inside Flagstaff House. Map L6

Exchange Square and Two IFC Tower

As the name suggests, Exchange Square houses Hong Kong's red-carpeted financial engine room, although the stock exchange is not open to visitors. However, the peaceful square outside it, dominated by a large fountain, is a great place to eat or drink outside. Near the fountain are sculptures by Henry Moore and Dame Elizabeth Frink. The square's tallest building, Two IFC Tower (see pp42–3), which was designed by Cesar Pelli, is an impressive landmark. Map L5

Former Government House

This grand old building served as the British governor's residence from 1855 until 1997, when the last governor, Chris Patten, handed Hong Kong back to China. Patten's successor, Tung Chee-hwa, cited bad feng shui created by the needle-like Bank of China building (see p42) as one reason not to move in, opting to remain in his house on the Peak. Back in the 1940s, the occupying Japanese added the Shinto-style towers to the Georgian structure, which at one time enjoyed harbour views. The building is used for official functions, only opening occasionally to the public – contact HKTB (see p139) for details. Map L6

The Escalator

A wonderful feature of Hong Kong is its 792-m- (2,598-ft-) long string of escalators, which links all the roads between Queen's Road and Conduit Street. It's the best way for pedestrians to get around the steep districts of Central, the Mid-Levels and SoHo. The Escalator runs uphill until midnight, except during the morning rush hour, when it runs downhill. Map K5

Frink sculpture, Exchange Square

For the top 10 sights from the Mid-Levels Escalator See p41

Left **Restaurant, SoHo** Right **Antiques, Hollywood Road**

SoHo
5 Since the late 1990s SoHo (so-called for being the area south of Hollywood Road) has been transformed from a sleepy district of traditional Chinese shops into a thriving area for hip bars, cafés and restaurants. Elgin, Shelley and Staunton streets are excellent places to find a drink or bite to eat. ◈ *Map K5*

Sheung Wan and Western
6 The older, more traditional Chinese areas of town, just west of Central's sleek corporate head-quarters and the smart shops, are worth exploring by foot. The reward is a fascinating array of shops, mostly wholesalers, selling dried seafood (the pervading smell here), ginseng, edible swallows' nests, snakes, arcane herbal ingredients and paper offerings for the dead. Try the streets around Bonham Strand. ◈ *Map J4*

Lan Kwai Fong
7 Not much to look at during the day, Lan Kwai Fong (or Orchid Square) only really starts to buzz at night when office workers, including plenty of city suits, come here to unwind at its many bars, clubs and rest-aurants. The street is packed with revellers on Fridays. The partying spills

Plague
In the 19th century, Hong Kong, like many other parts of the world in history, suffered devastating plagues incubated in filthy, crowded slums. It was also in Hong Kong where, in 1894, the source of the plague was identified, almost simultaneously, by two doctors. The discovery of the bacteria went on to revolutionize prevention and treatment of plague.

across to tiny Wing Wah Lane just across D'Aguilar Street with bars and good-value Thai, Malay and Indian restaurants. ◈ *Map K5*

The Waterfront
8 Turn right out of the Central Star Ferry for some (admittedly meagre and poorly exploited) open waterside space and benches with good views across

Man Mo Temple

 For Central's Statue Square **See pp10–11**

Laser and sound show at the Waterfront

to Kowloon. Behind is Jardine House, for many years Asia's tallest building. To the east is the giant upturned gin bottle shape of the Prince of Wales HQ building, which is now army barracks. The waterfront hosts the "Symphony of Lights" laser and sound show every evening at 8pm. Map L–M5

Man Mo Temple

The gloomy red and gold interior of the Man Mo Temple, dating back to the 1840s, is always thick with sandalwood smoke from the giant incense spirals hanging overhead, which take a couple of weeks to burn through. The temple is dedicated to two deities, Man (the god of literature) and Mo (the god of war). Some of the scenes from the film version of Richard Mason's *The World of Suzy Wong* were filmed here. Western end, Hollywood Rd • Map J5

Hollywood Road

This mecca for Chinese antiques and curios may no longer offer the bargains it once did but Hollywood Road's eastern end is still jammed with shops selling ancient ceramics, mammoth ivory carvings and delicate snuff bottles. The stalls and shops on Upper Lascar Row are a good hunting ground for antiques, trinkets, old coins, kitsch and curios. Some art galleries have also opened here. Map J–K5

A Day in Central

Morning

From Des Voeux Road take the tram westwards from Central and jump off outside the handsome colonial building housing **Western Market** (see p38). Browse among the ground floor trinkets or select a pattern from the many bolts of material on the first floor. The nearby Fung Shing restaurant serves excellent dim sum.

The streets around nearby Bonham Strand contain dried seafood shops, Chinese apothecaries, and paper offering shops. Head uphill to the atmospheric **Man Mo Temple**, then east past the antique shops of **Hollywood Road**, browsing as you go.

Break for lunch or a drink in one of the many restaurants and bars on the streets to the south (**SoHo**) or below Hollywood Road in **Lan Kwai Fong**.

Afternoon

Check out the fresh produce market stalls around the **Escalator** (see p59) and Graham Street before hitting **Statue Square** (see pp10–11), the Island's colonial heart.

Choose to visit the **upmarket malls** (see p63), or for some peace and harbour views head to Queen's Pier, or for altitude and a spectacular city perspective go up to the viewing gallery high in the imposing, needle-sleek **Bank of China Building** (see p42).

Quiet and shade are found in the nearby **Hong Kong Park** (see p59).

Left **St John's Cathedral** Centre **Colonial Police Station** Right **Legco Building**

Colonial Relics

St John's Cathedral
It may resemble a parish church more than a cathedral but St John's, completed in 1850, is the oldest Anglican church in east Asia. ⊗ *Map L6*

George VI Statue
This statue, erected in 1941 in the Zoological and Botanical Gardens, commemorates 100 years of British rule. ⊗ *Map K6*

Colonial Street Names
Most colonial buildings have been sacrificed to new development, but the colonial legacy is preserved in many of the roads named after royals (Queen's Road), politicians (Peel Street), military officers (D'Aguilar, Pedder) and public servants (Bonham, Des Voeux). ⊗ *Map K5–6*

Old Letter Box
A few traditional green, cast-iron post boxes bearing the British Royal Cipher remain. There is one at the northern end of Statue Square. ⊗ *Map L5*

Former Military Hospital
Broken into separate units – some abandoned – the huge, grand old building between Bowen and Borrett roads used to serve as a Military Hospital.
⊗ *Bowen Road • Map L6*

Hollywood Road Police Station
Bastions of colonial law and order, the Police Station (1864) and the old Victoria Prison (1841) still stand. ⊗ *Map K5*

Flagstaff House
Built in the mid-1840s, Flagstaff House is one of the oldest colonial buildings on the island and today houses the free teaware museum. ⊗ *Hong Kong Park • Map L6*

Duddell Street
While not spectacular, the gas lamps and old steps of Duddell Street date back to the 1920s. ⊗ *Off Ice House St • Map K5*

Legco Building
The elegant 1911 Neo-Classical building served as Hong Kong's Supreme Court and then as its Legislative HQ until 2011. The Legislative HQ is now located at Tamar. ⊗ *Map L5*

Mission Etrangères
The handsome former French Mission building (built 1917) is Hong Kong's Court of Final Appeal, though that's not an apt name given that the court has referred some legal wrangles to Beijing. ⊗ *Battery Path • Map L6*

Left **Harvey Nichols in the Landmark Centre** Right **Lane Crawford**

Up-Market Malls and Boutiques

The Landmark Centre
A smart, modern mall with conspicuous consumables from the likes of Chanel, Dior, Zegna, Versace, Prada, Vuitton, Bulgari and Tiffany. ◈ *Pedder St • Map L5*

Seibu
Four floors of designer clothes, cosmetics, gifts, household items and food. ◈ *Pacific Place, 88 Queensway, Admiralty • Map M6*

Lane Crawford
Upmarket clothing, with concessions from most big Western designer brands, houseware, beauty products, glass and porcelain, and Asia's largest female shoe shop. ◈ *Pacific Place, 88 Queensway, Admiralty • Map M6*

The Prince's Building
Not as many top names as the next-door Landmark, but the bright, airy and less crowded Prince's Building is worth a visit if big-name clothes and accessory designers are your thing. ◈ *Statue Square & Des Voeux Rd • Map L5*

G.O.D.
Goods of Desire is an ultra-hip store offering an off-beat selection of Chinese-inspired furnishings, accessories and clothing. ◈ *48 Hollywood Rd, Central • Map K5*

Gucci
This beautiful temple to the brand of Gucci is tended by elegant priestesses. It's merely a question of whether you can afford to worship here. ◈ *The Landmark Centre, G1 • Map L5*

Dragon Culture
Antiques shop with pottery from most dynasties, bamboo carvings and snuff bottles. ◈ *231 Hollywood Rd • Map K5*

Lock Cha Tea Shop
All the tea in China (well, 100 varieties anyway), along with traditional and modern teaware, all sold by experts in a colonial-era building. ◈ *G/F K.S.Lo Gallery, Hong Kong Park, Admiralty • Map L6*

Shanghai Tang
Local entrepreneur David Tang is behind this smart twist on traditional Chinese clothes and ornaments. Jackets and kitsch Mao watches are staples. ◈ *1 Duddell St, Central • Map K5–L5*

Two IFC
Hong Kong's smartest mall features a selection of top brands, including an Apple Store. There is also a Dymocks book shop, a superb supermarket and a cinema. ◈ *8 Finance St, Central • Map L4*

Left **The Globe** Right **Sevva**

🔟 Bars and Clubs

1 Dragon-i
The most happening club in Central, where models, movers and shakers, and celebrities from Jackie Chan to Sting, have been spotted. ⊗ *UG/F The Centrium, 60 Wyndham St • Map K5 • 3110 1222*

2 Café Gray Bar
This super swanky cocktail and wine lounge at the hip and swish Upper House Hotel has superb harbour views. ⊗ *49/F The Upper House Hotel, Pacific Place, 88 Queensway • Map M6 • 2918 1838*

3 One Fifth Nuevo
Unquestionably, this is one of Hong Kong's buzziest bars. Take in the fabulous crowd, soaring ceilings and big-city vibe. Also written as 1/5. ⊗ *9 Star St • Map K5 • 2529 2300*

4 V13
The enormous selection of flavoured vodkas will keep the most jaded of drinkers occupied. Raise a glass to the thirsty inmates of the Victoria Prison opposite. ⊗ *13 Old Bailey St • Map K5 • SoHo • 8208 1313*

5 The Globe
Hong Kong's best beer bar serves locally brewed microbeers and hard-to-find tap beers from around the world. ⊗ *45 Graham St, Central • Map K5 • 2543 1941*

6 Feather Boa
A former antique shop, now a bar, but with much of its old stock left in situ. Like drinking in a camp relative's front room. ⊗ *38 Staunton St, SoHo • Map 5 • 2857 2586*

7 Sevva
Bonnie Gokson's beautifully designed bar and restaurant is among the city's most stylish hangouts. ⊗ *25/F Prince's Building, 10 Chater Rd, Central • Map L5 • 2537 1388*

8 Beijing Club
Three floors of throbbing house, R&B and hip hop, through to as late (or early) as 9am *(see p52)*. ⊗ *2/F, 3/F & 5/F Wellington Place, 2–8 Wellington St, Central • Map K5 • 2526 8298*

9 Fringe Club
Hong Kong's alternative arts venue offers a respite from Lan Kwai Fong's rowdier beer halls. ⊗ *2 Lower Albert Rd, Central • Map K6 • 2521 7251*

10 Zoo Bar
Pioneering the trendification of this area, the Zoo Bar is a natural pit stop. It has a gay vibe, but straights are welcome. ⊗ *33 Jervois St, Western • Map K5 • 3583 1200*

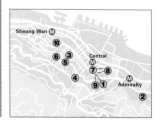

Price Categories

For a three-course meal for one with half a bottle of wine (or equivalent meal) and extra charges.

$	under HK$100
$$	HK$100–$250
$$$	HK$250–$450
$$$$	HK$450–$600
$$$$$	over HK$600

Lung King Heen

🔟 Restaurants

1 Lei Garden
This multi award-winning restaurant serves modern Cantonese as it should be – light, delicate and subtle. ⊗ *3/F IFC Mall • Map K5 • 2295 0238 • $$$*

2 The Mandarin Grill & Bar
The interior may have been revamped by Sir Terence Conran, but the menu still features English classics and premium seafood. ⊗ *Mandarin Oriental, 5 Connaught Rd • Map L5 • 2825 4004 • $$$$*

3 Island Tang
This elegant restaurant designed by Sir David Tang serves Cantonese dishes and Chinese *haute cuisine*. ⊗ *Shop 222, The Galleria, 9 Queen's Rd Central • Map L6 • 2526 8798 • $$$$*

4 8½ Otto e Mezzo Bombana
Three Michelin stars says it all, for this is Italian gastronomy of the highest quality *(see p48)*. ⊗ *202 Landmark Alexandria, 18 Chater Rd, Central • Map L5 • 2537 8859 • $$$$$*

5 L'Atelier de Joël Robuchon
Superstar chef Joël Robuchon picks up Michelin stars almost wherever he sets up a restaurant. Expect French classics *(see pp48–9)*. ⊗ *315 & 401 The Landmark, Central • Map L5 • 2166 9000 • $$$$$*

6 Lung King Heen
Executive chef Chan Yan Tak is the mastermind behind this contemporary Cantonese restaurant that has earned three Michelin stars *(see p49)*. ⊗ *Four Seasons Hotel, 8 Finance St, Central • Map L5 • 3196 8880 • $$$$$*

7 Jimmy's Kitchen
A favourite for its naff decor and retro menu, Jimmy's has been dishing out comfort food since 1928. ⊗ *1–3 Wyndham St • Map K5 • 2526 5293 • $$$*

8 Yung Kee
From its headset-toting waitresses to its efficient poultry kitchen (try the roast goose), Yung Kee is a riotous operation. ⊗ *32–40 Wellington St • Map K5 • 2522 1624 • $$$*

9 Caprice
Head chef Vincent Thierry and his team prepare modern French food in an open kitchen at this superb restaurant *(see p49)*. ⊗ *6/F Four Seasons Hotel, 8 Finance St • Map L5 • 3196 8860 • $$$$$*

10 Kau Kee
Humble Kau Kee was once offered millions for its beef brisket noodle recipe. Taste and see why. This is a place of pilgrimage. ⊗ *21 Gough St • Map J5 • 2815 0123 • No credit cards • $*

Left **Noonday gun** Right **Revolving restaurant, Hopewell Centre**

Hong Kong Island – Northeast

THE EAST OF THE ISLAND was the first to take up the population pressures of the nascent colonial capital of Victoria, and until the late 1970s had a low rent reputation. Some of that survives in the haggard pole-dancing clubs and tattoo parlours of Wan Chai, the quarter where Richard Mason wrote The World Of Suzie Wong, and where generations of sailors have nursed hangovers. But today, you're far more likely to run into Starbucks, serviced apartments and highly expensive office space. The night races at Happy Valley are where you'll see Hong Kongers at their most fevered, while in Causeway Bay is the neon of restaurants and boutiques. Further out, there are worthy surprises among the unlovely warehouses and office blocks of Quarry Bay and Chai Wan – live jazz, microbreweries and dance clubs.

Neon, "Old" Wan Chai

🔟 Sights in the Northeast

1. Central Plaza
2. Noonday Gun
3. Convention and Exhibition Centre
4. Lockhart Road
5. "Old" Wan Chai
6. Happy Valley Racecourse
7. Hopewell Centre
8. Victoria Park
9. Causeway Bay Typhoon Shelter
10. Tin Hau Temple

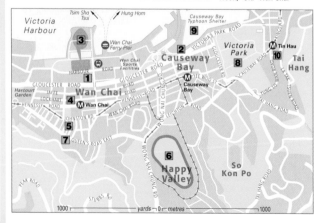

Share your travel recommendations on traveldk.com

Central Plaza

Central Plaza
Perhaps the developers figured "Central Plaza" had more cachet than "Wan Chai Plaza", or perhaps Wan Chai *is* more central than Central if you're talking about the mid-point of the waterfront. Anyway, Central Plaza is Hong Kong's third tallest building (after Two IFC Tower and the ICC Tower), standing at 374 m (1,227 ft). ◈ *18 Harbour Rd, Wan Chai • Map N5*

Noonday Gun
Immortalised in Noël Coward's famous song about *Mad Dogs and Englishmen,* the famous cannon has been fired at midday every day since 1860. Bigwigs pay for the privilege of firing it, with the money going to charity. Otherwise, a gunner dressed in traditional military attire does the honours. Originally it was fired whenever the Taipan arrived or departed from Hong Kong. ◈ *Waterfront near the Causeway Bay typhoon shelter • Map Q5 • To fire gun (for a fee): 2599 6111*

Convention and Exhibition Centre
The building looks a bit like the Sydney Opera House might if its roof had just been swatted by a giant hammer. The designers, however, maintain that the flowing lines are meant to evoke a bird in flight. It's certainly a study in contrast with the upthrust towers scratching the sky all around. There was a race against time to finish stage two of the $5 billion complex in time for the 1997 Handover ceremony. Britain's loss and China's gain is commemorated with a big black obelisk. The venue also hosts occasional raves and pop concerts. ◈ *1 Expo Drive, Wan Chai • Map N5 • 2582 8888*

Lockhart Road
Made famous in Richard Mason's novel *The World of Suzy Wong,* Wan Chai's sinful strip is these days an odd blend of girlie bars with doddery *mama-san* who saw action during the Vietnam War and will rob you blind as soon as look at you; down-at-heel discos; mock-British pubs; and super-trendy bars and restaurants. The road is almost always being dug up, adding to the hubbub. ◈ *Map M–P6*

Convention and Exhibition Centre

For more on modern buildings **See pp42–3**

Left **Happy Valley racing** Right **Hopewell Centre**

"Old" Wan Chai

This could almost be labelled Hong Kong's "Little Thailand". Dozens of Thai mini-marts and hole-in-the-wall Thai restaurants have sprung up amid Wan Chai market in the narrow warren of lanes that run between Johnston Road and Queen's Road East. You can find the same dishes here for a quarter of what you'll pay in smart Thai restaurants just blocks away. ◎ Map N6

Happy Valley Racecourse

From September to June the thud of hooves on turf rings out most Wednesday nights from this famous racetrack – once a malaria-ridden swamp – where Hong Kong's gambling-mad public wager more money per meeting than at any other track in the world. (See pp12–13.)

Hopewell Centre

Construction mogul Gordon Wu has built roads in China and half-built a railway in Bangkok, but this remains his best-known erection. The 66-storey cylinder rears up behind Wan Chai, making diners dizzy in its revolving restaurant, R66. The food, frankly, is not up to much, but the view

Victoria Park

makes up for it. Night-times are most spectacular – enjoy a cocktail as the sun dips behind the harbour. ◎ 183 Queen's Rd East, Wan Chai • Map N6 • R66: 2527 7292

Victoria Park

Hong Kong's largest urban park opened in 1957, and features a bronze statue of the killjoy British monarch, which one "art activist" once redecorated with a can of red paint. There's a swimming pool, tennis courts and lawn bowling greens. It's also the

Causeway Bay

venue for the Chinese New Year Flower Market, and every Sunday at noon would-be politicians can stand up and shoot their mouths off at the forum. ✎ *Map Q–R5*

9 Causeway Bay Typhoon Shelter

Barnacle-encrusted hulks and down-at-heel gin palaces rub gunwales with multi-million dollar yachts in this packed haven from the "big winds" that regularly bear down on the South China coast. There are also quaint houseboats with homely touches like flower boxes permanently anchored behind the stone breakwater. The impressive edifice to the left as you look out to sea is the Hong Kong Yacht Club. ✎ *Map Q5*

10 Tin Hau Temple

Not the biggest or best-known temple to the Chinese sea goddess but certainly the most accessible on Hong Kong Island. Worth a look if you're in the area. This was once the waterfront, believe it or not. There's usually a handful of worshippers burning incense and paying respects, although it may be packed during Chinese festivals. ✎ *Map R6*

A Day for Exploring

Morning

🕐 Start off with a brisk stroll through **Hong Kong Park**, a green haven surrounded on all sides by thrusting towers of glass and concrete. Chances are you'll see several caparisoned couples awaiting their turn to be married at the Cotton Tree Drive Registry Office. Take time for a look through the Edward Youde Aviary, a spectacular creation of mesh arches replete with Southeast Asian birdlife.

Make your way down past Citibank's imposing black towers to **Pacific Place** *(see p63)* for a coffee and some window shopping. Keep heading towards the harbour and you'll see to your right the elegant sweep of the **Convention and Exhibition Centre** *(see p67)*. Enjoy the harbour panorama through soaring glass walls.

Afternoon

Return to Wan Chai for lunch. **Lockhart Road** *(see p67)* is as good a place as any. The sleazy joints are still slumbering, and there is decent pub grub, Thai, Mexican and Chinese food on offer *(see p71)*.

Hennessy Road is the place to jump on a tram to Causeway Bay, due east of Wan Chai, or you may prefer to go one stop on the MTR. If you want to go shopping, take the Times Square exit, and start exploring from there. Then leave the crush and chaos behind with a leisurely afternoon stroll through **Victoria Park**, and perhaps a cocktail in Totts, the eyrie atop the Excelsior hotel.

Around Hong Kong Island – Northeast

Left **Sogo** Right **Page One**

10 Places to Shop

Page One
The best bookshop in Hong Kong, not least because the books are all stacked facing outwards. Huge range of fiction and non-fiction at reasonable prices. ⚲ *9/F Times Square, 1 Matheson St, Causeway Bay • Map P6*

Jusco
One of Japan's biggest department store chains. Lower rents to the east of the island translate into cheaper fashion, food and household goods. ⚲ *Kornhill Plaza, 2 Kornhill Rd, Quarry Bay • Map F5*

Sogo
With a fine range of mostly Japanese goods, Sogo is very popular among locals, though not up to Seibu's standards *(see p63)* in the hipness stakes. ⚲ *555 Hennessy Rd, Causeway Bay • Map P6*

Island Beverley
An arcane arcade stuffed with tiny boutiques featuring the creations of talented young local designers. ⚲ *1 Great George St, Causeway Bay • Map Q5*

Mezzanine
Fashion designer to the stars Vivian Luk has opened her own couture store offering Oscar-style gowns and dresses for women. ⚲ *13–15 Yik Yam St, Happy Valley • Map E5*

J-01
This store is cool bordering on crazy. The highlight of the hip and happening design collections is the "Splatter Collection" by Japanese artist Dehara Yukinori. It's hard to say if he's trying to be comical or is seriously deranged. Either way, don't miss his lurid, twisted figurines such as *Killed Person* and *Brainman*. ⚲ *57 Paterson St, Causeway Bay • Map Q5*

Spring Garden Lane
Head to this fun market for export-quality clothing at rock-bottom prices. ⚲ *Spring Garden Lane, Wan Chai • Map N6*

i.t.
Avant-garde fashions by young Asian designers. ⚲ *501, 5/F Times Square, Causeway Bay • Map P6*

Fortress
This is the best place to buy the latest electronics, which are sold at reasonable prices and with reliable guarantees. ⚲ *7/F & 8/F Times Square, 1 Matheson St, Causeway Bay • Map P6*

Lee Gardens
Prada, Paul Smith, Versace, Christian Dior and Cartier for the well-heeled. ⚲ *33 Hysan Ave, Causeway Bay • Map Q6*

Price Categories

For a three-course meal for one with half a bottle of wine (or equivalent meal) and extra charges.	**$** under HK$100
	$$ HK$100–$250
	$$$ HK$250–$450
	$$$$ HK$450–$600
	$$$$$ over HK$600

Joe Bananas

🔟 Places to Eat and Drink

1 Tasty Congee and Noodle Wantun Shop

For many this is the best place to go for beef fried noodles and piping-hot congee (rice porridge). The dim sum are also highly rated. ◈ G/F, 21 King Kwong St, Happy Valley • 2838 3922 • $

2 Petrus

With one Michelin star, Petrus serves contemporary French cuisine and boasts panoramic harbour views. ◈ Island Shangri-La, Supreme Court Road, Pacific Place • Map M6 • 2820 8590 • $$$$

3 Joe Bananas

Notorious meat market by night, good tapas by day. Avoid during Rugby Sevens week (see p37). ◈ 23 Luard Rd, Wan Chai • Map N6 • 2861 3776 • $$$

4 Vertigo Ultralounge

This swish cocktail lounge and nightclub is famed for its lavish interiors and DJ sets. ◈ 26/F QRE Plaza, 202 Queen's Rd East, Wan Chai • Map N6 • 2575 8980 • $$$

5 Yat Tung Heen

Drawing a strong local crowd, this Cantonese restaurant with one Michelin star is famed for its soups and seafood dishes. ◈ 2/F Great Eagle Centre, 23 Harbour Rd, Wan Chai • Map N5 • 2878 1212 • $$$$

6 American Peking Restaurant

Opened in the 1950s and still going strong. The name was a trick to attract US servicemen on leave during the Korean War. Excellent Peking duck. ◈ 20 Lockhart Rd • Map N6 • 2527 1000 • $$

7 The Pawn

This popular old Chinese pawn-brokers, converted into a bar-restaurant, has atmosphere in spades. Serves modern British cuisine. ◈ 62 Johnston Rd, Wan Chai • Map N6 • 2866 3444 • $$$$

8 Bo Innovation

Awarded two Michelin stars, this highly modern Chinese restaurant attracts a hip clientele. ◈ 2/F J Residence, 60 Johnston Rd, Wan Chai • Map N6 • 2850 8371 • $$$$

9 One Harbour Road

For Cantonese food at its most pure and subtle, with no fusion or foreign influences, head to One Harbour Road. ◈ Grand Hyatt, 1 Harbour Rd, Wan Chai • Map N5 • 2584 7722 • $$$$

10 Brown

Happy Valley has also been taken over by a host of trendy wine bars and eateries. The decor is, well, brown. ◈ 18A Sing Woo Rd • 2891 8558 • $$

Left **Giant panda, Ocean Park** Right **Floating Restaurants**

Hong Kong Island – South

DESPITE THE SLOW CREEP OF FLOODLIT HOUSING ESTATES *to the east and west, the south of Hong Kong Island (or "Southside" as everyone calls it) retains more than enough rugged coastline, wooded upland and sequestered beach to startle anyone whose preconception of Hong Kong was wholly urban. Traffic from the city passes through the Aberdeen Tunnel and enters a bright and shiny landscape of golf clubs, marinas and opulent homes. There is good swimming at Repulse and Deep Water bays, and even, at Big Wave Bay, some acceptable surf. Over at Stanley, stallholders set out their coral beads and antique opium pipes, while at isolated Shek O, media types and young commuters snap up beachfront village houses. The Dragon's Back ridge, plunging down the southeast corner, offers some of the island's best walking, with views of the South China Sea.*

🔟 Sights in the South

1. Aberdeen Harbour
2. Floating Restaurants
3. Ocean Park
4. Deep Water Bay
5. Repulse Bay
6. Shek O
7. The Dragon's Back
8. Stanley
9. Ap Lei Chau
10. Chinese Cemetery

Ocean Park

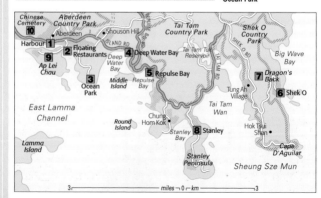

Aberdeen Harbour

good view of the harbour, boats and boatyards. However, when you want to eat, take a ferry from Aberdeen to Lamma Island's many seafood restaurants instead *(see p117)*. ◈ *Map E5*

Aberdeen Harbour

Residential blocks crowd Aberdeen's small, lovely harbour, which is still filled with high-prowed wooden fishing boats despite the fact that overfishing and pollution have decimated the Hong Kong fishing industry. Ignore the ugly town centre and instead photograph the tyre-festooned sampans, or walk to the busy wholesale fish market at the western end of the harbour and watch the catches being loaded onto trucks and vans. ◈ *Map E5*

Floating Restaurants

Also in Aberdeen Harbour are two giant floating restaurants, which are popular but garish, production-line eateries. The most famous, The Jumbo, is said to have served more than 30 million people. Prices are not especially attractive, nor are the culinary achievements. Free ferries shuttle between these restaurants, and pushy sampan handlers also lie in wait for meandering tourists. Take one of these boats if you want to get a

Ocean Park

This long-established theme park responded to the arrival of Disneyland on Lantau Island with a major refurbishment and a corresponding surge in popularity. There's enough to keep children and adults alike busy for a whole day. More than 30 permanent rides and animal attractions range from rollercoaster rides to giant pandas and great aquatic displays, such as Atoll Reef, which recreates the habitats and sealife of a coral reef *(see also p54)*.
◈ *Map E5 • 3923 2323 • www.oceanpark. com.hk • 10am–6pm daily • Adm*

Deep Water Bay

There's an almost Mediterranean air to the lovely beach and waterfront of Deep Water Bay, a popular place for beach lovers and the well-to-do who settle in the Bay's upmarket housing. The smallish beach is protected by lifeguards and a sharknet, and the water is usually clean. As with most beaches in Hong Kong, it gets crowded in fine weather.
◈ *Map E5*

Left **Fish market, Aberdeen Harbour** Centre **Aquarium, Ocean Park** Right **Deep Water Bay**

Left **Repulse Bay** Right **Shek O**

Repulse Bay

Another popular destination, Repulse Bay's beach is clean and well-tended, if sometimes over-crowded with thousands of visitors. Eating and drinking choices range from small cafés on the beach to the Verandah *(see p77)*, a classy restaurant run by the same group as the Peninsula Hotel in Tsim Sha Tsui. Try afternoon tea here. The Hong Kong Life Guards Club at the far southern end of the beach is also worth a look for its scores of statues of gods and fabulous beasts. ◈ *Map F5*

Shek O

Remote and undeveloped, the village of Shek O is worth the relatively lengthy train and bus ride necessary to reach it. The serenity is upset only at weekends by droves of sun worshippers heading for its lovely beach. A short walk to the small headland leads to striking rock formations, pounding waves and cooling South China Sea breezes. Surfing and body boarding

House by the sea, Shek O

The Defence of Hong Kong

The British made sure that Hong Kong was well defended from the sea, but it was always vulnerable to attack from the north. During World War II, the island fell to a Japanese attack via the mainland. Hundreds of civilians were interned in Stanley prison, and the well-kept cemetery nearby is the resting place of many who died either trying to defend Hong Kong or during the occupation.

---

are often viable on Big Wave Bay, a short walk or taxi ride north. Head to the Black Sheep *(see p77)*, a lovely bar and Mediter-ranean-style restaurant, for a post-ramble beer and a bite to eat. ◈ *Map F5*

The Dragon's Back

This 4-mile (6-km) walk looks daunting on the map, but the route along the gently ascending ridge of the Dragon's Back will not mean too much huffing and puffing for the reasonably fit. The reward is unbeatable views down to the craggy coastline of the D'Aguilar Peninsula, Big Wave Bay and genteel Shek O. At a gentle pace the walk should take about three hours, enough time to build up a good appetite when you arrive in Shek O. Take plenty of water. ◈ *Map F5*

Stanley

A former fishing village, Stanley was one of the largest towns on the island before the British arrived and placed a fort on its strategic peninsula. Relics from both eras remain, but Stanley's many excellent seafront restaurants and its extensive market are justifiably the main draws for visitors (see pp16–17).

Ap Lei Chau

Supposedly the most densely populated island in the world, Ap Lei Chau (or Duck Tongue Island), opposite the Aberdeen waterfront, is crowded with high-rise developments. Bargain hunters may find a visit to the discount outlets at the southern end of the island worthwhile (see p76). Close to the ferry pier are some small family businesses, boatyards and temples that have survived the modern developments.
Map E5

Chinese Cemetery

Chinese Cemetery

Stretching away on the hill above Aberdeen, the Chinese Cemetery is a great place for photographs, both of the cemetery itself and of the harbour beneath. Negotiating the steep, seemingly endless steps is quite an undertaking, though, especially on a hot day.
Map E5

A Circular Tour

Morning

This circular tour of Hong Kong Island is perfectly feasible to complete in a day, so long as you don't start too late.

From Central, jump on an Aberdeen-bound bus, alighting close to **Aberdeen harbour** (see p73). Haggle for a sampan harbour tour offered by one of the pushy touts on the waterfront. Don't expect an informative commentary. Keep a look out for Aberdeen's few remaining houseboats.

Avoid the production-line floating restaurants and opt instead for lunch at **Repulse Bay**, which is just a 15-minute bus ride away. Enjoy the beach and a swim, then take lunch either at one of the beachfront cafés or the upmarket **Verandah** (see p77). Alternatively, head to the supermarket behind the Verandah and create your own picnic.

Afternoon

Just a short hop further south along the coast, the lovely town of **Stanley** is certainly worth a visit. If you haven't yet eaten, the restaurants here are excellent, some with lovely sea views. Lose a couple of hours browsing for clothes and souvenirs in **Stanley market**, though admittedly it is not Hong Kong's best market (see p39).

If you want to get some walking in, take a short bus or taxi ride to Tai Tam country park. A path leads through to Wong Nai Chung Gap, from where buses and taxis head back into the city.

Around Hong Kong Island – South

Left **Sale signs at an outlet store** Right **The Birdcage**

Designer Outlets in Ap Lei Chau

Horizon Plaza
This shabby, high-rise building on the edge of the island of Ap Lei Chau *(see p75)* is home to a number of outlets for discount clothing, warehouse furniture, antiques and home furnishings. A taxi from Aberdeen is probably the simplest way to reach it. ✪ *2 Lee Wing St, Ap Lei Chau • Map E5*

Joyce Warehouse
The extensive selection of clearance designer wear from the stores of Hong Kong chain Joyce are perhaps the main reward for struggling out to Horizon Plaza *(above)*. You get discounts of 60 per cent on the likes of Armani. ✪ *21/F Horizon Plaza*

Replay
A samples and warehouse shop with limited stocks of casual clothes, but great discounts, often around 80 per cent. ✪ *19/F Horizon Plaza*

Inside
A modest warehouse outlet of a smart interior furnishings chain. There's a small range of clearance items at discounts that can be as high as 90 per cent. ✪ *12/F Horizon Plaza*

The Birdcage
This one offers mostly original Chinese antiques and curios sourced by the owners of the Birdcage shop on the mainland. Items range from portable antiques and curios to furniture. ✪ *22/F Horizon Plaza*

i.t.
Off-season contemporary fashion lines by emerging Asian designers are sold here at discount prices. ✪ *5/F Horizon Plaza*

Lane Crawford Outlet
Slow-moving items and old stock from Hong Kong's trendy department store are on sale here at much lower than orginal prices. ✪ *25/F Horizon Plaza*

Matahari
Chinese antiques and reproductions, soft furnishings, silk Shanghai-style lamps and hand-painted children's furniture are crammed into Matahari's extensive store and wholesale warehouse. ✪ *11/F Horizon Plaza*

Space
Take your pick of last season's bags, accessories, shoes and clothes by the inimitable Italian designer Miuccia Prada. Minimalist decor and layout ensure a true Prada experience. ✪ *2/F East Commercial Block, Marina Square, South Horizons*

Golden Flamingo
Lots of smaller knick-knacks alongside the bigger ticket furniture at Golden Flamingo include a wide selection of attractive Chinese vases, picture frames and lacquer jewel boxes. ✪ *27/F Horizon Plaza*

Price Categories

For a three-course meal for one with half a bottle of wine (or equivalent meal) and extra charges.

$	under HK$100
$$	HK$100–$250
$$$	HK$250–$450
$$$$	HK$450–$600
$$$$$	over HK$600

Saigon at Stanley

🔟 Places to Eat and Drink

The Verandah
Indisputably Southside's premier venue, the Verandah, with its candlelight, sea views and old colonial grandeur, is the place for big-budget romancing. ◈ 109 Repulse Bay Rd, Repulse Bay • Map F5 • 2292 2879 • $$$$

The Black Sheep
Stroll the quiet lanes of the bohemian enclave of Shek O on the southeast coast, and this veggie-friendly, organic café beckons. ◈ 330 Shek O Rd, Shek O Village • Map F5 • 2809 2021 • $$$

Pickled Pelican
Reliable, tasty English pub food is served with speciality beers and a wide choice of Scotch whiskies here. ◈ 90 Stanley Main St, Stanley • Map F6 • 2813 4313 • $$$

Spices
One of the best places for alfresco dining in Hong Kong, Spices serves well-executed Thai and Indian curries in a lush garden setting. It has a relaxed atmosphere and good service. ◈ G/F The Repulse Bay Hotel, 109 Repulse Bay Rd, Repulse Bay • Map F5 • 2292 2821 • $$$

The Boathouse
Service could be better, but you are here to sit upstairs or at the pavement tables with views out to sea, eating the pub-style seafood. The fish and chips won't disappoint. ◈ 88 Main St, Stanley • Map F6 • 2813 4467 • $$$

Saigon at Stanley
End a satisfying day in Stanley at this atmospheric Vietnamese restaurant. Romantics will gravitate towards the balcony tables at sunset. ◈ 101 Murray House, Stanley Plaza • Map F6 • 2899 0999 • $$$

Top Deck
Residents usually avoid the floating restaurants as most of them are tourist traps, but the revamp of Jumbo's top floor has brought the crowds back. The seafood buffet is excellent (see p49). ◈ Top Floor, Jumbo Kingdom, Shum Wan Pier Drive, Aberdeen • Map E5 • 2552 3331 • $$$

Coco Thai
Romantic, low-key beachside place to eat Thai food whilst gazing out to sea. At its best in the evenings. ◈ Island Rd, Deepwater Bay • Map E5 • 2812 1826 • $$

Smuggler's Inn
Stanley's gentrification has thankfully bypassed the Smuggler's Inn, which is a relic of the days when British soldiers from Stanley Fort blew half their wages here. ◈ 90A Stanley Main St • Map F6 • 2813 8852 • $$

Lucy's
Perennially popular venue for bistro-style nosh, with Mediterranean influences. Vibes are relaxed, standards consistently above par. Stanley's answer to a light, well-bred lunch. ◈ 64 Stanley Main St • Map F6 • 2813 9055 • $$$

Following pages **Plover Cove, the New Territories**

77

Left **Cultural Centre** Centre **Oysters, Sheraton Hotel** Right **Gargoyle, Boom Bar**

Kowloon – Tsim Sha Tsui

O N ONE LEVEL, *Tsim Sha Tsui (universally truncated to "TST" in a merciful gesture to non-Cantonese speakers) is still a parody of a tourist quarter in an Asian port: its tailors and camera salesmen do not suffer fools, its hostess bars are the scene of many a ruinous round of drinks. But there is also much more to TST than that. There is a profusion of world-class cultural venues, galleries and museums. There are hotels – the Peninsula, the Inter-Continental, the Langham – of jaw-dropping luxury. And in the monolith that is Harbour City is every product and service the human mind can conceive of.*

Peninsula Hotel

Sights in TST

1 The Golden Mile
2 The Peninsula Hotel
3 Museum of History
4 Space Museum
5 Science Museum
6 Museum of Art
7 Kowloon Mosque
8 Cultural Centre
9 Clocktower
10 Kowloon Park

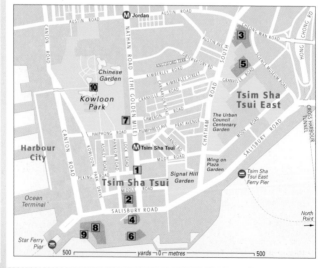

Share your travel recommendations on traveldk.com

The Golden Mile

special offers sometimes apply. A night in the opulent Peninsula suite will set you back the price of a new car. It boasts eight bars and restaurants, including the Philippe Starck-designed Felix and cognoscenti-favoured Gaddi's *(see p87)*. If you desire, you can swoop onto the roof by helicopter or be collected by Rolls-Royce *(see also p147)*. ◈ *Salisbury Rd, Kowloon • Map N4 • 2920 2888*

The Golden Mile

This strip that stretches up Nathan Road from the waterfront could be more accurately dubbed the "neon mile". It's less glitzy than Central and comprises mainly bars, restaurants, tailors, camera and electronic shops and the odd desultory topless bar. The crowds are so great that walking the Golden Mile becomes a major challenge. ◈ *Map N1–4*

The Peninsula Hotel

The last word in luxury accommodation and service. This venerable hotel sits like a proud old dowager, gazing sedately across at the vertiginous Hong Kong Island skyline. The cheapest rooms start where many other luxury hotels stop, although

Museum of History

This museum was built at a cost of almost HK$400 million, half of which was spent on its *pièce de résistance*, the Hong Kong Story, which attempts to chronicle the 400 million-odd years since Hong Kong coalesced from the primordial ooze. The story is told across eight galleries containing more than 4,000 exhibits, which vividly outline the natural environment, folk culture and historical development of Hong Kong. ◈ *100 Chatham Rd South • Map M3 • 2724 9042 • 10am–6pm Mon & Wed–Sat, 10am–7pm Sun • Adm (free Wed)*

Space Museum

When you've had enough of history, come and peek into the future. This odd-looking dome in the heart of Tsim Sha Tsui includes an omnimax theatre and interactive exhibits such as the jetpack ride. ◈ *Cultural Centre Complex, 10 Salisbury Rd • Map N4 • 2721 0226 • 10am–9pm Sat & Sun, 1–9pm Mon & Wed–Fri • Adm (free Wed)*

Left **Museum of History** Right **Space Museum**

Left **Science Museum** Right **Cultural Centre**

Science Museum

5 Some fascinating interactive displays here if you don't mind fighting your way through the giggling, pushing throngs of schoolchildren. There are enough buttons to push, gadgets to grapple with and levers to tweak to satisfy even the most hard-to-please kids. Basic principles of chemistry, physics, biology and other sciences are explained but in a much more entertaining and less dry manner than in the class-room. ◎ *2 Science Museum Rd • Map P3 • 2732 3232 • 10am–9pm Sat & Sun, 1–9pm Mon–Wed & Fri • Adm (free Wed)*

Museum of Art

6 You may well be fed up with museums by this point. If not, here you'll find oil paintings, etchings, lithographs and calligraphy. One display features pottery shards and suchlike from southern China dating back to Neolithic times, and there is also a fine collection of elegant porcelain from various Chinese dynasties. ◎ *10 Salisbury Rd • Map N4 • 2721 0116 • 10am–6pm Fri–Wed (to 8pm Sat) • Adm (free on Wed)*

Museum of Art

Chungking Mansions

This grim and squalid collection of guesthouses, flops and fleapits amid the glitter of Nathan Road has become the stuff of legend over the years, resisting attempts to knock it down. The bottom three floors are full of fabric shops, fast-food joints and lurid video shops. You may trip over a collapsed drug addict in amongst the rats and firetrap wiring. Hong Kong auteur Wong Kar-wai made this the setting of his 1994 hit film, *Chungking Express*. The best way to experience the Mansions is in one of the cheap Indian restaurants.

Kowloon Mosque

7 When the muezzin calls the faithful to prayer, the Jamia Masjid Islamic Centre is where you'll find most of Hong Kong's Muslims. You can stop by for a look, but take your shoes off and be respectful. Entry to the inner part is not permitted unless you are a Muslim come for prayer. ◎ *105 Nathan Rd • Map N3 • 2724 0095 • 5am–10pm daily • Jumah (Friday) prayers at 1:15pm*

Cultural Centre

8 With a peerless view beckon-ing across the water, the geniuses in charge decided to build the world's first windowless building, and covered it for good measure in pink public toilet-style tiles. Wander around and marvel at one of the great architectural

debacles of the 20th century. That said, it hosts some good dance and theatre. ◎ 10 Salisbury Rd • Map M–N4 • 2734 9009 • 9am–11pm daily, Box office 10am–9.30pm daily

Clocktower

Clocktower

The Kowloon-Canton Railway, which now ends at Hung Hom, used to finish at this clocktower, as did the rather more famous Orient Express (see also p14). An extension now brings trains once again to the tip of Kowloon. From here, you can walk for more than a kilometre around the TST waterfront and marvel at the odd optimistic fisherman dangling a line in the harbour. ◎ Map M4

Kowloon Park

While in TST, if you feel one more whisper of "Copy watch? Tailor?" may provoke you to irrational violence, then venture through the park gates, find a well-shaded bench and watch the world go by. There's a big swimming pool (reputed to be something of a gay cruising zone), an aviary and a pond featuring flamingos and other aquatic birdlife. ◎ Haiphong Rd • Map M–N3 • 5am–midnight daily

Kowloon Park

A Morning Out

Early Morning

Catch the **Star Ferry** (see pp14–15) to TST. As you come in, check out the vast West Kowloon Reclamation site to the left, home of the shiny, silver International Commerce Centre Tower. The 118-floor monolith houses hotels, apartments and a viewing deck.

If you're still standing after the stampede to disembark (be wary of pyjama-clad old ladies), saunter past the old **clocktower**, pause to take in one of the world's most breathtaking views, then cross Salisbury Road and stop for tea at the **Peninsula Hotel** (see p81).

From here, brave the crush and bustle of the **Golden Mile** (see p81). Unless you want a new suit or dress, do not make eye contact with the legion of touts who have never heard the word "no". Walk straight by. They are merciless if they sense weakness.

Brunch

When you've had enough of the smog-shrouded streets, hawkers and being jostled, cross Haiphong Road into **Kowloon Park**. There is plenty of space here to pause and do some serious people-watching.

You'll probably be getting peckish by now. Head back down Nathan Road to Joyce Café, for reasonably priced vegetarian fare and an earful of *tai-tais* (wealthy housewives) comparing the morning's purchases. The espressos and capuccinos are first-rate; the vegetable lasagna delicious.

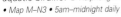

Left **Chungking Mansions** Centre **Kowloon Park** Right **The Langham Hotel**

🔟 Spots to People-Watch

1 Tao Heung
Come here early and join the Cantonese at their best – tucking into a tasty, fresh and made-to-order dim sum breakfast with their families, or just sitting quietly with a pot of tea and a newspaper. ◈ 3/F Silvercord Centre, 30 Canton Rd • Map M3 • 2375 9128 • $$

2 Chungking Mansions
Hours of harmless fun to be had watching the endless stream of freaks, geeks and desperados being accosted by a legion of touts (see pp82 & 152).

3 Mirador Mansions
Not as famous as its above-mentioned neighbour, but entertaining nonetheless. More weirdos. More confused backpackers. ◈ 54–64 Nathan Rd • Map N4

4 Kowloon Park
Best spot is on the benches near the fountain in the centre of the park. In summer, there is a constant and colourful procession along the path (see p83).

5 Felix
If the wallet won't stand up to a meal, just drink in the bar and watch everyone watching everyone else (see p87).

6 Harbour City
A people-watcher's paradise. Massive labyrinth of interconnected malls with plenty of cafés and benches to park upon and soak up the orgy of conspicuous consumption (see opposite).

7 Waterfront Promenade
Walking east from the Star Ferry you will meet Tai Chi adepts, culture vultures and local ladies with their tiny dogs. The promenade is very popular for the harbour's Symphony of Lights show, which takes place at 8pm daily. ◈ Salisbury Rd • Map M4–N4

8 The Langham Hotel
Understated and elegant, the Langham attracts clientele of the same ilk, such as screen star Michelle Yeoh, perhaps on her way to T'ang Court. ◈ 8 Peking Rd • 2375 1133 • Map M4

9 Star Ferry Pier
This perenially busy ferry pier is the place to watch ferries and their passengers. ◈ Map M4

10 Heritage 1881
Heritage 1881 is the name given to the super-swanky, revamped former Hong Kong Marine Police headquarters. It features a boutique hotel, bars and restaurants, and designer shops. ◈ 2A Canton Rd • Map M4

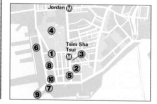

Left **Harbour City shopping mall** Right **Joyce**

🔟 Places to Shop

Harbour City
There are at least 700 shops in this vast agglomeration of malls stretching the length of Canton Road. It comprises the Ocean Terminal, Ocean Centre and Golden Gateway complexes. For serious shoppers only. ◈ *Canton Rd • Map M3–4*

Granville Road
Great for souvenir T-shirts, all manner of big-label knock-offs and factory seconds. Also top value at chain stores like Bossini and Giordano. ◈ *Map N3*

Joyce
Founder Joyce Ma is a Hong Kong icon. Her flagship store is in Central, but the Nathan Road outlet is also impressive. ◈ *Glo Gateway Centre, Canton Rd • Map N4*

Rise Commercial Building
It doesn't look much from outside, but inside this mall you will discover a trendsetter's utopia. ◈ *Cnr Chatham Rd South and Granville Rd • Map N3*

Beverley Centre
This was the original beacon of cool in TST. Floor after floor of mini-boutiques from young local designers. ◈ *87–105 Chatham Rd South • Map N3*

The Peninsula Hong Kong Arcade
A selection of fashionable designer boutiques, jewellers and bespoke tailors is located in the Peninsula Hotel *(see p81)*. ◈ *Salisbury Rd, Kowloon • Map M4*

Star House
Top place for computers, software and all things geeky. Don't be afraid to bargain. ◈ *3 Salisbury Rd • Map M4*

Toys 'R' Us
Probably their biggest branch in Hong Kong. Kids will love it, your bank manager may not. ◈ *Shop OTG23 G/F, Ocean Centre • Map M4*

Fortress
If you're after electronic goods and baffled by the sheer number of shops around TST, chain store Fortress is a good bet. Other shops may advertise cheaper prices, but not all dealers are honest. ◈ *Shop 335–7, Level 3, Ocean Centre • Map M4*

Sam's Tailor
Portraits of former clients, including princes, presidents and pop stars, look on as the third generation of the Melwani family measures you for a well-priced, well-fitting suit that will be ready in two to three days. ◈ *Burlington Arcade, 94 Nathan Rd • Map N3*

Left **Sky Lounge** Right **The Lobby Lounge**

TOP10 Places to Drink

Aqua Spirit
Sit in a cubbyhole facing the window and sip a glass of bubbly as you watch the harbour light up. ❧ 29/F, 1 Peking Rd • Map M4

The Lobby Lounge
Some of the best harbour views in Hong Kong are to be found in the lobby of the superb Hotel InterContinental (see also p147). They are well worth the price of the drinks. ❧ 18 Salisbury Rd • Map N4

Mes Amis
A long list of wines by the glass and a full supporting cocktail menu make this bar popular with visitors and locals alike. There's a busy ladies' night on Wednesdays. ❧ G/F 15 Ashley Rd • Map N4

The Bar
This upscale watering hole serves as a delightful refuge from the crowds – but prepare to pay through the nose for drinks. ❧ 1/F The Peninsula • Map N4

McLovin's Tavern
More than just your average city Irish bar, this excellent watering hole serves Italian and Mexican food in addition to ales and bar snacks. ❧ G6 Tsim Sha Tsui Centre, 66 Mody Rd • Map P3

Dada Lounge
A gorgeous cocktail and wine bar, Dada Lounge is decorated in truly over-the-top style with Alice in Wonderland outsize chairs, chandeliers and horsehead motifs. ❧ 2/F De Luxe Manor, 39 Kimberley Rd • Map N3

Manchester United Bar
Whether you are a fan of the footballing Red Devils or not, this pleasantly upscale bar offers a friendly vibe and a mixed clientele. Famous ex-footballers occasionally drop in for a pint. ❧ 32–34 Lock Rd • Map N3

Fatt's Place
This casual beer bar has a great selection of international and local ales. ❧ 2 Hart Ave • Map N3

Sky Lounge
Another very comfortable, tower-top location from which to enjoy the nightly cross-harbour light show with a glass of something chilled to hand. ❧ Sheraton Hotel, 20 Nathan Rd • Map N4

Ned Kelly's Last Stand
This place has been here forever, as has the jazz band. An opportunity to get your feet tapping to tunes by the crustiest, most grizzled bunch of musicians this side of New Orleans. ❧ 11A Ashley Rd • Map N3

Recommend your favourite bar on traveldk.com

Price Categories

For a three-course meal for one with half a bottle of wine (or equivalent meal) and extra charges.

$	under HK$100
$$	HK$100–$250
$$$	HK$250–$450
$$$$	HK$450–$600
$$$$$	over HK$600

Morton's of Chicago

TOP 10 Places to Eat

Oyster and Wine Bar
Sublime view and oysters so fresh they flinch when you squeeze a lemon on them. ◈ *18/F Sheraton Hotel, 20 Nathan Rd • Map N4 • 2369 1111 • $$$$$*

Felix
The food is fantastic, the view better and the bar crammed with the rich and famous. Check out the cheeky Philippe Starck-designed urinals, where you relieve yourself against a glass wall and feel like you're showering Hong Kong. ◈ *28/F The Peninsula • Map N4 • 2696 6778 • $$$$$*

Morton's of Chicago
Carnivore's paradise. Huge slabs of cow, aged and cooked to perfection. ◈ *4/F Sheraton Hotel • Map N4 • 2732 2343 • $$$$$*

Cuisine, Cuisine
Michelin-starred Cantonese cuisine fuses traditional and modern styles in an elegant setting. ◈ *The Mira Hotel, 118 Nathan Rd • Map N3 • 2368 1111 • $$$$*

Wildfire
A great place for pizza and pasta, Wildfire has terrace seating at the front and a rear courtyard garden. It is a popular weekend brunch spot. ◈ *2 Knutsford Tce • Map N3 • 3690 1598 • $$$*

Gaddi's
Impeccable French cuisine, irreproachable service and famous patrons have earned Gaddi's its reputation as one of Asia's finest restaurants *(see p48)*. ◈ *1/F The Peninsula • Map N4 • 2696 6763 • $$$$$*

Delaney's
Reasonably authentic Irish menu and great range of draught ales and whiskeys. Also lots of dim lighting and cosy nooks. ◈ *Basement, 71–77 Peking Rd • Map N4 • 2301 3980 • $$*

Nobu
Enjoy fine dining at one of the world's most famous Japanese restaurants. ◈ *2/F InterContinental Hotel, 18 Salisbury Rd • Map N4 • 2313 2323 • $$$$$*

Spoon
Another superlative Alain Ducasse restaurant. Even the 550 spoons suspended from the ceiling are unlikely to distract you from the best French food in town. ◈ *Hotel InterContinental, 18 Salisbury Rd • Map N4 • 2313 2256 • $$$$$*

Hutong
Updated Northern Chinese classics are served in this theatrically lit restaurant with magnificent views. ◈ *28/F, 1 Peking Rd • Map M4 • 3428 8342 • $$$$*

Left **Kowloon waterfront** Centre **Market stall, Reclamation Street** Right **Bird-lover**

Kowloon – Yau Ma Tei, Mong Kok and Prince Edward

GRITTY, PROLETARIAN AND UTTERLY ENGROSSING, *Yau Ma Tei and Mong Kok* provide a heady mix of karaoke bars, dodgy doorways and street markets before terminating in the more upscale apartments of Prince Edward. If Hong Kong has an emotional heartland, then it is these hectic streets, every paving slab the scene of some delicious hustle. Within living memory there were open fields here, but now all is uncompromising Cantonese ghetto. Come for some of Hong Kong's best shopping, restaurants of rowdy authenticity and a sensuous barrage that will linger in your mind.

🔟 Sights

1. Bird Garden
2. Flower Market
3. Tin Hau Temple
4. Temple Street Night Market
5. Jade Market
6. Ladies Market
7. West Kowloon Reclamation
8. Boundary Street
9. Shanghai Street
10. Reclamation Street Market

Façade detail, Tin Hau temple

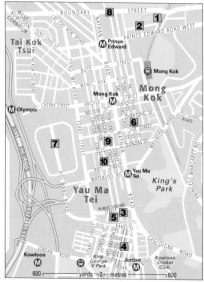

Temple Street

Bird Garden

Bird Garden

The small but pretty Bird Garden is where local folk, mostly elderly, take their birds to sing and get some fresh air. There's also a small bird market here selling sparrows, finches and songbirds in elegant little cages. Fresh bird food, in the form of live grasshoppers, is fed to the birds through the cage bars with chopsticks. ◈ *Yum Po St*

Flower Market

Near the Bird Garden is a vibrant flower market, at its best and brightest in the morning. The stalls and shops lining the entire length of Flower Market Road sell a wide variety of exotic flowers – a wonderfully colourful sight and a good place to take photographs. The busy market is especially exciting to visit during the Chinese New Year *(see p36)*. ◈ *Flower Market Rd*

Tin Hau Temple

The Tin Hau temple in Yau Ma Tei is divided into three sections. Only one of these is actually devoted to Tin Hau, the sea goddess who is Hong Kong's favourite deity and essentially its patron. Admittedly, it is neither the oldest nor the grandest temple in the territory, but it is pretty nonetheless. The other two sections are dedicated to Shing Wong, the god of the city, and To Tei, the god of the earth. Officially no photography is allowed anywhere inside the temple. English-speaking visitors should head for a couple of stalls at the far end of the temple, where they can have their fortunes told in English. ◈ *Map M1 • 8am–5pm daily*

Temple Street Night Market

Visit the chaotic, crowded night market on Temple Street as much for the spectacle as for the shopping *(see pp18–19)*.

Left **Flower market** Right **Tin Hau temple**

For more about Hong Kong's markets See pp38–9

Left **Quiet lane near Yau Ma Tei's Tin Hau Temple** Centre **Jade for sale** Right **Shanghai Street**

Jade Market

The small, covered Jade Market is worth a quick forage even if you're not intending to buy any jade. Dozens of stalls sell jewellery, small animals (many representing characters from the Chinese zodiac) and beads in jade. There will be few bargains on sale, particularly to those without a knowledge of good jade, but there's plenty of cheap jade here if you just want to own some trinkets. 🔍 Kansu St • Map M1

Ladies Market

The term "ladies" is somewhat out of date, as there's plenty more than women's clothing here. The shopping area consists of three parallel streets: Fa Yuen Street, crammed mostly with sports goods and trainer shops; Tung Choi Street (the former ladies market); and Sa Yeung Choi Street, specializing in consumer electronics. Market stall prices are cheap, and shop prices are better than those on Hong Kong Island. The crowds here can be tiring, though, especially on hot days. 🔍 Map E4

West Kowloon Reclamation

The reclaimed land of West Kowloon is a jumble of road

The Triads

Overcrowded Mong Kok is the heartland of the Hong Kong triad gangs. The triads originated in 17th-century China as secret societies who tried to reinstall the Ming dynasty after the Manchus took over. Though they have been given a romantic image in literature and the cinema, the modern-day reality is of sleaze and slayings. Tourists are unlikely to be a target, however, so don't be put off visiting this exciting district of Hong Kong.

intersections and messy building sites, as planners argue over exactly what will fill it. Rising 484 m (1,588 ft) over everything, the International Commerce Centre opened in 2010 as the tallest building in Hong Kong, topping Two IFC. Its sky100 Observation Deck provides the highest indoor viewing point in the city. 🔍 Map L1–3

Boundary Street

History is visible in the ruler-straight line of Boundary Street, which marked the border between British Hong Kong and China between 1860 and 1898. The lower part of the Kowloon Peninsula was ceded (supposedly in perpetuity) by China to the British, who wanted extra land for army training and commerce. The British then became worried over water shortages and wanted yet more land to protect Hong Kong Island from the threat of bombardment from newly invented long-range artillery. In 1898 the border was moved again to include the entire New Territories, this time on a 99-year lease *(see p30)*. ◈ Map E4

Shanghai Street

The whole area around Shanghai and Reclamation streets is a traditional Chinese neighbourhood, if somewhat less vibrant and seedier than it once was. Interesting nooks and shops include funeral parlours, herbalists, health tea shops, paper kite shops and, at 21 Ning Po Street, a shop selling pickled snakes. ◈ Map E4

Reclamation Street Market

If you haven't seen a Hong Kong produce market in full swing, you could do worse than wander down Reclamation Street. This predominantly fruit and vegetable market will provide some good photo opportunities. The squeamish, however, may want to avoid wandering inside the municipal wet market building where livestock is freshly slaughtered and expertly eviscerated on the spot. ◈ Map E4

Homeware shop, Shanghai Street

Down the Peninsula

Early Morning

🕐 Take the MTR to Prince Edward to start at the top of the Kowloon Peninsula, near the old Chinese border at **Boundary Street**. Take Exit B2 and head to the **Bird Garden** via the flower shops and stalls on **Flower Market Road** *(see p89)*. Testament to the Chinese love of exotic goldfish, the stalls at the top of Tung Choi Street sell a surprising variety of shapes and colours.

Cheap shops and market stalls abound a short walk away to the south on the streets below Argyle Street and east of Nathan Road. Pedestrians also abound – some 150,000 souls live in every square kilometre of this part of the Peninsula.

Crossing Nathan Road, head to the **Jade Market** for jewellery and figurines. If you want the best choice of jade, arrive before lunchtime because some of the stallholders pack up after this.

Early Afternoon

Take a breather in the small, pleasant square across the way and watch the world go by with the elderly locals, or peep inside the busy **Tin Hau Temple** *(see p89)*. Then break for a rough and ready cheap Chinese lunch in the covered canteens on the corner of Pak Hoi and Temple streets.

After lunch explore the produce stalls along **Reclamation Street** and the old Chinese district around **Shanghai Street**.

Left **Chan Chi Kee Cutlery** Right **Sasa Cosmetics on Nathan Road**

🔟 Funky Shops

1 King Wah Building
Head to this uncrowded mall for funky street clothing, great accessories, handbags and cool watches. There's genuine vintage denim and other 1970s and 1980s rarities, plus kitsch Japanese cartoon ephemera aplenty. ◐ 628 Nathan Rd

2 i.t.
This smart, minimalist outlet stocks sleek Japanese and American street clothes and accessories. ◐ 2/F IN's Square, 26 Sai Yeung Choi St

3 Izzue
Another good place for hepcats and urban warriors to find the right tops and dancing trousers for a night out. ◐ 1/F IN's Square, 26 Sai Yeung Choi St

4 Sony Pro Shops
Head to the Sony Vaio, Walkman and PlayStation Pro Shops for the latest audio and video gems among Sim City's computer shops. ◐ Sim City, Chung Kiu Commercial Building, 47–51 Shan Tung St

5 Mongkok Computer Centre
The deals on computer hardware and software are not as good as those in Sham Shui Po, but this is convenient for a huge selection of games and accessories. ◐ 8A Nelson St

6 Sasa Cosmetics
Conveniently located outlet of an extensive Hong Kong chain selling cosmetics of every shade and type at very low prices. Perfume is a bargain here. ◐ Bank Centre Mall, 636 Nathan Rd

7 Ban Fan Floriculture
The porcelain and ceramic vases and wicker-work flower baskets are not likely to win awards for chic or design, but the choice is impressive and the prices are reasonable. ◐ 28 Flower Market Rd

8 Chan Chi Kee Cutlery
Cheap, sturdy woks, steamers, choppers and pretty much everything else you might desire for the well-equipped kitchen. ◐ 316–318 Shanghai St

9 Sandy Chung
Your one-stop shop in the jade market for pearls, beads and jewellery of all sorts. Go between 11am and 4pm. ◐ Jade Market stall 413–414, Kansu St

10 Fa Yuen Commercial Building
Audio and videophiles will be in their element here, among the very latest in sleek gadgets at competitive prices. ◐ 75–77 Fa Yuen St

Left **Saint's Alp Teahouse** Right **The Lobby Lounge**

🔟 Cheap and Chinese Eats

Majesty Seafood
This bright, informal restaurant serves excellent, inexpensive dim sum breakfasts. 🔊 3/F Wu Sang House, 655 Nathan Rd • Map E4 • 2397 3822 • $$

Tai Ping Koon
Hong Kong's version of western food at a branch of a century-old chain. Try the "Swiss" (sweet) sauce chicken. 🔊 19–21 Mau Lam St • 2384 3385 • $$

Mui Chai Kee
A great stop for a pot of tea and some fruit jellies and lotus paste buns. The adventurous might try the bird's nest and egg tarts or double boiled frog's oviduct with coconut milk. 🔊 G/F 120 Parkes St • Map N2 • 2782 7301 • No credit cards • $

Peking Restaurant
Peking duck is the speciality, or try Yangzhou fried rice with ham and peas at this gently ageing, charming restaurant. 🔊 I/F 227 Nathan Rd • Map N2 • 2735 1316 • No credit cards • $$

Saint's Alp Teahouse
Quirky snacks and an intriguing menu of teas in a modern Taiwan-style Chinese teahouse, which is one of an extensive chain. 🔊 61A Shantung St • 2782 1438 • No credit cards • $

Tim Ho Wan
Crowds queue up for the Michelin star-rated lotus-leaf rice packets, cha siu pastries, persimmon cakes and fun gwor dumplings served here. 🔊 Taui Yuen Mansion 2, 2–20 Kwong Wa St, Mong Kok • Map E4 • 2332 2896 • $

Ah Long Pakistan Halal Food
A good bet if you fancy a spicy curry, although the surroundings aren't pretty. 🔊 G/F Tak Lee Bldg, 95B Woosung St • Map N2 • 2782 1635 • No credit cards • $$

Fairwood
Part of a large Chinese fast-food chain, this branch has CD listening posts and some Internet terminals. 🔊 B/F King Wah Centre, 620–628 Nathan Rd • 2302 1003 • No credit cards • $$

The Lobby Lounge
Deserves a mention for its glass atrium, outdoor seating, terrific coffee and afternoon tea menus. 🔊 4/F The Eaton Hotel, 380 Nathan Rd • Map N1 • 2710 1863 • $$

Light Vegetarian
Familiar mock-meat dishes on the à la carte menu, but the real steal is the ample lunchtime buffet, which includes desserts and a pot of tea. 🔊 13 Jordan Rd • Map N2 • 2384 2833 • No credit cards • $

Left **Temple prayer sticks and incense** Right **Lion Rock**

New Kowloon

THE SITE OF THE OLD AIRPORT, *Kai Tak has not been allowed to lie fallow, with the former terminal converted into the world's largest golf driving range. In the neighbouring streets are excellent budget dining and seconds outlets, for this is where locals go bargain-hunting. Culture is found to the north, in the Tang Dynasty-style architecture of the Chi Lin Nunnery or the joyful chaos of Wong Tai Sin Temple.*

🔟 Sights in New Kowloon

1. Wong Tai Sin Temple
2. Lion Rock
3. Kowloon Walled City Park
4. Oriental Golf City
5. Chi Lin Nunnery
6. Lei Yue Mun
7. Fat Jong Temple
8. Lei Chung Uk Tomb
9. Hau Wong Temple
10. Apliu Street

Kowloon Walled City Park

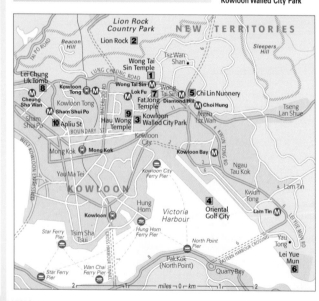

Left **Smoky offerings** Right **Wong Tai Sin Temple**

Wong Tai Sin Temple

A noisy, colourful affair, Wong Tai Sin is always crowded and aswirl with incense smoke. Legend holds that Wong Tai Sin (originally known as Huang Chu-ping), who was born in Zhejiang Province around AD 328, could see the future and make wishes come true. The temple opened in 1921, after a Taoist priest brought a sacred portrait of Huang to Hong Kong. Its vivid, stylised architecture contrasts sharply with the surrounding concrete boxes. Worshippers from the three main Chinese religions – Taoism, Buddhism and Confucianism – flock here, not to mention 100-odd soothsayers hawking their services. Find out for yourself if they are as accurate as Huang. Behind the temple is an ancient and mysterious tomb that still baffles historians. ◈ Map F4
• 7am–5:30pm

Lion Rock

One of the best places to view this fascinating natural landmark is, conveniently, from outside Wong Tai Sin temple. Find the open area near the fortune tellers' stalls where you can look straight up at what from this angle resembles the grizzled head of a male lion. Those feeling energetic may be tempted to scale its heights. Take lots of water, and be warned – the top section is not for the faint-hearted. ◈ Map E4

Kowloon Walled City Park

One of Hong Kong's most picturesque parks began life in 1847 as a Chinese fort. A legal oversight by the British left the fort under Chinese control after the New Territories were leased to Britain. It was levelled during World War II, and a labyrinthine ghetto called the Walled City sprang up in its place. This bizarre place quickly became a magnet for triads, drug dealers, heroin addicts, pornographers and rats the size of small dogs (see p96). It was pulled down in 1992 and replaced by the park. A display of photographs in the almshouse near the entrance tells the story. ◈ Map E4

Maze, Kowloon Walled City Park

Oriental Golf City

This is, reputedly, the world's biggest driving range, with more than 200 bays. Whack away to your heart's content – unless you're well-connected or seriously rich, this is as close as you'll get to a golf course in Hong Kong. ◈ Kai Tak Runway, Kai Fuk Rd • Map F4
• 2522 2111 • 7am–midnight • Adm

Chi Lin Nunnery

Chi Lin Nunnery

It is said that not a single nail was used in the construction of this lavish replica of a Tang Dynasty (AD 618–907) place of worship. The nunnery opened in 2000, funded by donations from wealthy families. Hall and side wings house impressive statues, including those of Sakyamuni Buddha and the Boddhisatva Guanyin. Do not miss the gorgeous, tranquil Nan Lian Gardens opposite, similarly designed around Tang Dynasty principles: artfully arranged rocks, trees, bridges and wooden pavilions successfully conceal the location in the middle of a busy traffic circle. ⬔ *Chi Lin Drive, Diamond Hill • Map F4 • 9am–4:30pm Thu–Tue • Free*

Lei Yue Mun

Once a fishing village, Lei Yue Mun translates as "carp gate", although the only fish you're likely to see now are in the excellent seafood restaurants

> ### The Grimmest Conditions on the Planet
>
> More than 50,000 poor souls once inhabited the Kowloon Walled City *(see p95)*, a place of few laws and no taxes, but plenty of diseases and desperate criminals. In the 1950s the triads moved in, and the narrow lanes often ran red with blood. Before 1992 it was also one of the few places left in Hong Kong to find grizzled opium addicts puffing away in divans.

lining the waterfront. This is the closest point between Hong Kong Island and Kowloon but don't be tempted to swim across – if the pollution doesn't kill you, you'll be whisked away by the strong currents. ⬔ *Map F5*

Fat Jong Temple

Although it is one of the most famous Buddhist sites in Hong Kong, the Fat Jong Temple is little visited by foreigners. Making it well worth the journey to see

Left **Chi Lin Nunnery complex** Right **Lei Yue Mun fish market**

is the striking colour scheme – with red pillars standing out from the white walls – ornate decorations and magnificent Buddha sculptures. The temple somehow manages to be be both busy and serene at the same time. ◈ 175 Shatin Pass Rd, Won Tai Sin • Map E4 • 10am–6:30pm. Closed Mon

Lei Cheng Uk Tomb
The Han burial tomb (AD 24–220) can barely be seen through a scratched sheet of perspex. Still, it's one of Hong Kong's earliest surviving historical monuments, so act impressed. ◈ 41 Tonkin St, Sham Shui Po • Map E4 • 10am–6pm Mon–Wed, Fri & Sat; 1–6pm Sun • Free

Hau Wong Temple
Quaint and tiny, Hau Wong is hardly worth a special trip, but take a look if you're in the area. It was built in 1737 as a monument to the exiled boy-emperor Ping's most loyal advisor. Usually fairly quiet unless a festival is in full swing. ◈ Junction Rd • Map E4 • 8am–5pm daily

Apliu Street
This huge street market is full of all sorts of strange junk and pirated goods. You'll feel you're on another planet here – this is as "local" as Hong Kong gets. It includes perhaps the world's biggest collection of secondhand electrical stuff. Occasionally you can spot the odd retro turntable or radio, but most of it is rubbish. ◈ Map E4

Apliu Street

An Afternoon Out

After Lunch

Catch the MTR to **Wong Tai Sin** (see p95) and brave the crowds of earnest worshippers at the temple. Some of the fortune tellers in the nearby stalls speak English. Try to bargain them down to a third or quarter of the price given. Some use numbered sticks, others prefer curved bits of wood known as Buddha's lips.

If you're feeling fit, tackle **Lion Rock** (see p95). It's a demanding climb, but the views are superb. The steep inclines towards the top are for the stout of heart only. Take plenty of water on a warm day.

A 10-minute taxi ride will take you to the **Kowloon Walled City Park**, Hong Kong's loveliest urban park. The tranquil green space contains eight different gardens.

Late Afternoon

By late afternoon you should have worked up an appetite, so take a cab to the seafood restaurants on the waterfront at **Lei Yue Mun**. Watch the sun paint the skyscrapers pink and orange as it sinks into the harbour, while you crack open crabs and munch on giant shrimps, all washed down with wine or an icy Tsing Tao beer.

With two huge stone lions guarding its front door, one restaurant that is difficult to miss while strolling around Lei Yue Mun is **Kong Lung Seafood** (see p99). Here you can feast on a range of seafood dishes, including deep-roasted crab and steamed abalone with orange crust.

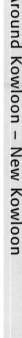

Left **Dragon Centre** Centre **Page One** Right **Festival Walk shopping mall**

TOP10 Places to Shop

Golden Shopping Centre
Cheap computer equipment here, and nearby shops have a massive range of VCDs and DVDs. Take care – many are poor-quality pirate recordings. ◈ *94A Yen Chow St, Sham Shui Po • Map E4*

Dragon Centre
Soaring glassy mall in the midst of Sham Shui Po's grime and dust. Good food hall, computer stuff and a terrifying rollercoaster. ◈ *37K Yen Chou St cnr Cheung Sha Wan Rd, Sham Shui Po • Map E4*

Hong Kong Records
This stylish record and CD shop – the kind that almost seems obsolete in today's "download" world – is always busy with young and old music lovers. ◈ *Shop L2–01, Festival Walk, Kowloon Tong • Map E4*

Yuet Chung China Works
The place to come for all kinds of china objects – tableware, decorative, personalized or monogrammed. Orders may take four weeks but shipping is arranged. ◈ *3/F Kowloon Bay Industrial Centre, 15 Wang Hoi Rd, Kowloon Bay • Map F4*

Lancôme
Take your pick from the skin check-up, the 45-minute VIP consultation, or go straight for a one-hour facial in a private cabin. ◈ *G18 Festival Walk, Kowloon Tong • Map E4 • 2265 8665*

Page One
A massive branch of Hong Kong's great bookshop chain, this gets top marks for stacking books with the covers facing outward, saving readers badly kinked necks. It has a good coffee shop, too. ◈ *Shop LG1–30, Festival Walk, Kowloon Tong • Map E4*

Yu Chau Street and Nam Cheong Street
The small shops that line these two streets sell an enormous range of laces, zippers, ribbons, beads and buttons – a wider choice than you might have imagined could exist. ◈ *Map E4*

Crabtree and Evelyn
More sweet-smelling goodies to pamper yourself with here. The smell of lavender pot-pourri nearly knocks you over as you step over the threshold. ◈ *Shop UG17, Festival Walk, Kowloon Tong • Map E4*

Bang & Olufsen
Audiophiles will drool over the sleek designs and crystal clarity from one of the most distinguished names in sound. ◈ *Shop LG1–10, Festival Walk, Kowloon Tong • Map E4*

Belle
The largest retailer of women's shoes in China has outlets in Hong Kong. It stocks a great range of shoes, particularly its own label. ◈ *112 Level 1, Plaza Hollywood, Diamond Hill • Map E4*

Price Categories

For a three-course meal for one with half a bottle of wine (or equivalent meal) and extra charges.

$	under HK$100
$$	HK$100–$250
$$$	HK$250–$450
$$$$	HK$450–$600
$$$$$	over HK$600

Amaroni's Little Italy

🔟 Places to Eat and Drink

1 Cambo Thai
Kowloon City is famous for its cheap and tasty Thai food. Be warned that you may need a couple of beers to put out the fire from the beef salad. ✆ *25 Nga Tsin Long Rd, Kowloon City • Map E4 • 2716 7318 • $$*

2 agnès b. Délices
The French fashion chain has opened a classy chocolate store and café. A heaven for chocoholics, it serves the sweetest treats in the area. ✆ *UG-20 Festival Walk, Kowloon Tong • Map E4 • 2265 8990 • $$*

3 Exp
The health-conscious will be pleased to find unexpected combinations of tried and tested noodles with offbeat additions such as grapefruit. ✆ *UG23 Festival Walk, Kowloon Tong • Map E4 • 2265 8298 • $$*

4 Chong Fat Chiu Chow Restaurant
If you want to try traditional Chiu Chow seafood this restaurant serves some of the best. Go for the crab or goose dishes. ✆ *60–62 South Wall Rd, Kowloon City • Map E4 • 2383 3114 • $$*

5 Wing Lai Yuen Sichuan Noodles
Traditional Sichuan food in a plain setting. The dan dan noodles are the most delicious thing on the menu. ✆ *1/F Site 8 Whampoa Garden • Map E4 • 2320 6430 • $$$*

6 Amaroni's Little Italy
Hong Kongers love Italian, and they have taken this place to heart. Share plates and make yourself at home. ✆ *Shop LG1–32 Festival Walk, Kowloon Tong • Map E4 • 2265 8818 • $$$*

7 Tso Choi Koon
Literally "rough food", this is one for those prepared to take some culinary risks to experience the real Hong Kong. Are you up to sauteed pig's intestines and fried pig's brains? ✆ *17–19A Nga Tsin Wai Rd, Kowloon City • Map E4 • 2383 7170 • No credit cards • $$*

8 Festive China
In fact, the festivities are fairly muted here, but the food is good. Northern-style Chinese cooking and glossy interiors. ✆ *Shop LG1 Festival Walk, Kowloon Tong • Map E4 • 2180 8908 • $$$*

9 House of Canton
The full range of Cantonese dishes, from shark's fin and abalone to an exhaustive assortment of dim sum snacks are available here. ✆ *LG/F 240 Festival Walk, Kowloon Tong • Map E4 • 2265 7888 • $$$*

10 Kong Lung Seafood
You can't miss this place – two huge stone lions guard the front door. Deep-roasted crab and steamed abalone with orange crust rate highly. ✆ *62 Hoi Pong Rd West, Lei Yue Mun • Map F4 • 2775 1552 • $$$*

Note: Unless otherwise stated, all restaurants accept credit cards

Left **Stairs to Ten Thousand Buddhas Monastery** Centre **Railway Museum** Right **Lek Yuen Bridge**

The New Territories

*A*S A NAME, THE NEW TERRITORIES *is suggestive of frontier country; in colonial times this was indeed the place where pith-helmeted sahibs went on tiger shoots, threw tennis parties and wrote memoirs. Today, much of it is suburban rather than rural: more than a third of Hong Kong's population lives here, in dormitory towns dotted across "the NT", as locals abbreviate it. But to the north are Hong Kong's largest expanses of open country, including the important Mai Po marshes, and there are centuries-old temples and settlements. At the NT's northern extremity is the border with "mainland" China.*

NT Sights

1. Ten Thousand Buddhas Monastery
2. Sha Tin Racecourse
3. Amah Rock
4. Hong Kong Railway Museum
5. Ching Chung Koon
6. Kadoorie Farm
7. Heritage Museum
8. Yuen Yuen Institute
9. Tin Hau Temple
10. Castle Peak Monastery

Left **Amah Rock** Centre **Racegoer, Sha Tin** Right **Pagoda, Ten Thousand Buddhas Monastery**

Images, Ten Thousand Buddhas Monastery

afternoons between September and June. The racecourse was redeveloped for the 2008 Olympics so that the dressage and show jumping events could be held here. ◈ *Map F3 • Racecourse MTR • 2695 6223 • www.sha-tin.com • No children • Adm*

Ten Thousand Buddhas Monastery

The Buddhas in question are stacked on shelves in the main hall of this hillside sanctuary at Pai Tau Tsuen, Sha Tin. In fact, there are more like 13,000 Buddha images now. The monastery comprises five temples, two pavilions and an elegant nine-storey pagoda. Take a deep breath before you enter the grounds – there are 400-odd steps to negotiate. ◈ *Map E3 • East Rail Line to Sha Tin, take north exit and follow signs • 9am–5pm • Free*

Sha Tin Racecourse

Hong Kong's most famous horseracing track is at Hong Kong Island's Happy Valley *(see pp12–13)*, but the people who live in this part of the world are so mad about horseracing they built a second racetrack in the NT. More than 85,000 punters have been known to pack Sha Tin's $500-million world-class track, where record-breaking sums are wagered on Saturday and Sunday

Amah Rock

An odd tower of rocks near Lion Rock Tunnel that when viewed from a certain angle, looks eerily like a woman with a baby on her back, hence the name. Legend holds that the amah's husband sailed overseas to find work, while she waited patiently for his return. When a storm sank his boat, she was so grief-stricken she turned to stone. An alternative interpretation is that the rock was created as an ancient phallic symbol. ◈ *Map E4 • East Rail Line to Tai Wai*

Hong Kong Railway Museum

Tai Po's museum is not one of Hong Kong's best, but train-spotters will like it. Old coaches sit on tracks outside what used to be Tai Po Market Station. Inside is a tolerably interesting account of the city. Guided tours are also available. ◈ *13 Shung Tak St, Tai Po • Map E2 • East Rail Line to Tai Po Market, then follow signs • 2653 3455 • 9am–5pm. Closed Tue • Free*

Left **Sha Tin Racecourse** Right **Hong Kong Railway Museum**

Left **Ritual, Yuen Yuen Institute** Left **Mai Po marshes**

Ching Chung Koon

The temple's name means "evergreen pine tree", a symbol of longevity and perseverance. The Koon, a Taoist sect, built the first structure, the Palace of Pure Brightness, in 1961 and has since added pagodas, pavilions and gardens. There's also vegetarian food and a bonsai collection.
⊗ Tsing Chung Path, Tuen Mun • Map C3 • MTR to Siu Hong, then taxi or LRT 50S • 7am–6pm daily • Free

Kadoorie Farm

Set up by local moguls Lord Lawrence and Sir Horace Kadoorie in 1951 to provide work for some 300,000 penniless refugees, Kadoorie Farm and Botanic Garden is now a centre for conservation and environmental awareness, promoting biodiversity in Hong Kong. It includes a deer haven and butterfly house. ⊗ Lam Kam Rd, Tai Po • Map E2 • Bus 64K from Tai Po Market East Rail Line • 2483 7200 • www.kfbg.org.hk • Phone ahead for opening times • Adm

Heritage Museum

Saving the Sanctuary

The NT's Mai Po marshes *(see p44)* are a world-class site of ecological significance, with more than 60,000 birds stopping here on migratory routes each winter. Kingfishers, herons and cormorants abound, and the marshes are one of the last habitats for the near-extinct black-faced spoonbill and Saunders' gull. Hong Kong's premier birdwatchers' paradise has been the subject of fierce debate and hard-fought battles between staunch environmentalists and developers desperate for scarce new land. The environmentalists, fortunately, have the upper hand. The biggest danger is pollution and industrial waste seeping into the marshes from factories at nearby Deep Water Bay.

Heritage Museum

Sha Tin's museum vies with the revamped Museum of History in Kowloon for Hong Kong's best museum honours *(see pp20–21)*.

Yuen Yuen Institute

This temple complex is popular with Buddhists, Confucianists and Taoists alike. It's usually full of worshippers, so be respectful. The main building is a replica of Beijing's Temple of Heaven. The notices outside carry the latest soothsayers' wisdom on which

Yuen Yuen Institute

signs in the Chinese horoscope are set for an auspicious year. Try the tasty vegetarian food in the Institute's restaurant. ◈ *Map E3*
• *MTR to Tsuen Wan, then minibus 81*
• *2492 2220 • www.yuenyuen.org.hk*
• *8:30am–5pm daily • Free*

Tin Hau Temple

At the far end of Clearwater Bay sits the oldest of Hong Kong's temples dedicated to the sea goddess Tin Hau. It's eerily quiet as you descend through a patch of forest. Inside the temple, spirals of incense drop ash onto models of fishing boats. ◈ *Bus 91 from Diamond Hill, then minibus 18*
• *Map G3 • 7am–5pm daily • Free*

Castle Peak Monastery

The 1-mile (1.5-km) walk from the nearby light railway station is hard, but this is a nice little outing to relieve stress if the bustle of Hong Kong is getting to you. Suck in some (relatively) fresh sea air and let the chanting of the monks soothe your soul. ◈ *Map B3 • 9am–5pm daily • Free*

A Day in the NT

Morning

🕐 Take the MTR to Kowloon Tong, then switch to the East Rail Line train. Get off at Tai Po Market station, and take the 64K bus or a taxi to Lam Tsuen. This is home to the Wishing Trees, with auspicious red ribbons tied to their branches. Buy a red paper strip from nearby stalls, write down your wish, then affix it to the adjacent boards.

Head back to the East Rail Line, and proceed to Fanling station. Take the 54K bus to Lung Yeuk Tau, start of the **Lung Yeuk Tau Heritage Trail** *(see p104)*. This takes you through the five famous walled villages of the New Territories, built by ancient clans as safe havens from bandits. The walk takes a couple of hours, and provides a fascinating insight into what life once was like in these parts.

Afternoon

Take a bus or taxi back to the East Rail Line, and travel on to Sha Tin station. A short cab ride away is the **Lung Wah Hotel** on 22 Ha Wo Che Street which isn't a hotel any more, but a restaurant. This eating house has been going strong for more than 50 years, so they must be doing something right.

If you are in Sha Tin on a weekend between September and June, head off to the **racecourse** *(see p101)* for an afternoon of thundering hooves.

On weekdays or out of the racing season, check out Sha Tin's excellent **places to shop** at New Town Plaza *(see p106)*.

103

Left **Tsang Tai Uk** Centre **Fish restaurant, Sai Kung village** Right **Ruin, Fanling heritage trail**

🔟 Historic Villages and New Towns

Tsang Tai Uk
This stronghold of the Tsang clan dates back to 1848 and is built in typical Hakka style, with thick walls and a defensive tower in each corner. Dozens of families still live here. ⊗ *Map L3*

Tsuen Wan
This is the terminus of the MTR line and a perfect example of new town overcrowding. Worth a look just to glimpse Hong Kong life at its bleakest. ⊗ *Map D3*

Sha Tin
Less grim version of Tsuen Wan, with a massive shopping centre. Home to Hong Kong's second racetrack. ⊗ *Map E3*

Fanling
Fanling's Tang Chung Ling ancestral hall belongs to the foremost clan in the New Territories. The Lung Yeuk Tau heritage trail is nearby. ⊗ *Map E2*

Sheung Shui
Home to another of the main local clans the Liu. From here, it's a quick cab ride to Lok Ma Chau, one of the border crossings, where the architects-on-acid skyline of Shenzhen

Warrior image, Fanling

looms through the pall. Another ancestral hall. ⊗ *Map E1*

Sai Kung
Quaint fishing village turned expatriate haunt. Pubs with names like Steamers and the Duke of York, offset by old Chinese men click-clacking mahjong tiles in tiny cafés. ⊗ *Map G3*

Kam Tin
The name means "brocade field", although these days any crops are more likely to be decorated with rusty cars. Traditional walled villages at Kat Hing Wai and Shui Tau. ⊗ *Map C3*

Ping Kong
Off the beaten track, and therefore its walled village is less busy than others. ⊗ *Map E1*

Tap Mun Chau
One of the New Territories' best-kept secrets. Picturesque little island where villagers watch the world go by from quaint homes. ⊗ *Map H2*
• *Ferry 8:30am–6:30pm*

Tai Po
Its market and Railway Museum are worth a quick look, before making your way to scenic Plover Cove. ⊗ *Map E2*

Kam Tin river

Left **Plover Cove** Right **San Mun Tsai floating village**

🔟 Areas of Natural Beauty

Plover Cove
This isn't actually a cove, at least, not any more. In fact it's a massive reservoir which was created by building a dam across the mouth of the bay, then pumping all the seawater out and pumping in fresh water from China. Hike or bike the trails. Maps from HKTB. ✎ *Map F1*

Bride's Pool
Stunning waterfalls amid lush forest. Take the camera and wear sensible shoes. ✎ *Map F2*

Tai Po Kau
Forest reserve near the Chinese University, popular with serious birdwatchers. ✎ *Map F2*

San Mun Tsai
Charming village perched between verdant hills and a sparkling bay. Check out the local fisherfolks' floating homes with their dodgy wiring. ✎ *Map F2*

Tai Mo Shan
"Big fog-shrouded mountain" is the translation, although on many days the peak of Hong Kong's tallest mountain is visible. It reaches 957 m (3,139 ft). Quite a hike to the top, but superb views await the intrepid. ✎ *Map D3*

Mai Po Marsh
The marsh on the western edge of the New Territories is a bird sanctuary *(see p44)*. ✎ *Map D2*

Clearwater Bay
Various walks and beaches on offer here. From Tai Au Mun, you can walk to the less than inspiringly named Clearwater Bay Beach One and Beach Two or Lung Ha Wan (Lobster Bay). Shark sightings send the locals into a lather each summer, and in the past holes have been found in some nets. You've been warned. ✎ *Map G5*

Long Ke Wan
Relatively inaccessible little gem of a beach. Don't get too carried away with the view as you descend the vertiginous goat track, or you may find yourself at the bottom sooner than you intended. ✎ *Map H3*

Tai Long Wan
Hong Kong's finest beach, on the beautiful Sai Kung Peninsula. Take a good map and lots of fluids before setting off *(see pp22–3)*. ✎ *Map H3*

Ma On Shan
The mountain's name means "saddle", a reference to its shape *(see p45)*. ✎ *Map F3*

Tai Long Wan

Around the Region – The New Territories

Left **Bossini** Right **Universal Models**

TOP 10 Places to Shop

1 IKEA
Even those who are not normally fans of the Swedish chain will find the wide array of made-in-China goods attractive. ◈ *L6 HomeSquare, 138 Sha Tin Rural Committee Rd, Sha Tin • Map F3*

2 My Jewellery
Innovative designs and prices that won't break the bank. Check out their diamond-studded chokers. ◈ *Shop 15, Citylink Plaza, Sha Tin • Map E3*

3 Universal Models
There's plenty here for the model enthusiast, whether you're after incredibly detailed military figurines or the latest Mobile Set Gundam. An added attraction for some is a scary range of pellet-firing replica guns. ◈ *603–609 Castle Peak Rd, Kong Nam Industrial Building, Tsuen Wan • Map E4*

4 Tai Po's Produce Markets
Tai Po is packed with atmospheric markets; those outside Fu Shin Street's Man Mo temple are the best. ◈ *East Rail Line to Tai Po Market Station, then follow signs to temple • Map E2*

5 Overjoy Porcelain Factory
There are hundreds of patterns on offer, making this the perfect place to buy your dinner service. ◈ *1/F Block B, Kwai Hing Industrial Building, Kwai Chung • Map E3 • 2487 0610*

6 Suzuya
Cute, girly Japanese fashion label. Just the ticket if you want to look like Sailormoon or Hello Kitty. ◈ *Shop 462, 4/F New Town Plaza, Sha Tin • Map E3*

7 Bossini
Big branch of the cut-price chain store. Stock up on comfy cotton T-shirts, socks and khakis. ◈ *Shop 307, 3/F New Town Plaza, Sha Tin • Map E3*

8 Marks & Spencer
Sensible shoes, comfortable underwear and comfort food for homesick Britons. One of their biggest Hong Kong branches. ◈ *Shop 329–39, 3/F New Town Plaza, Sha Tin • Map E3*

9 Hang Heung Bakery
Hong Kong's most popular baker of "wife cakes", a flaky pastry filled with red bean paste. These traditional confections are *de rigueur* at Chinese weddings. ◈ *64–6 Castle Peak Rd • Map C2*

10 Wing Wah Bakery
Hong Kong's premier purveyor of moon cakes *(see p50)*. These rich glazed pastry treats are eaten during the Mid-Autumn festival. The egg yolks in the centre represent the full moon, although you can get cakes with fruit fillings instead. ◈ *86 Castle Peak Rd • Map C2*

Children outside Bossini

Left **Shoppers, New Town Plaza** Centre **Hebe One O One** Right **Regal Riverside Hotel**

Places to Drink

Steamers
Make merry at Sai Kung's most stylish pub, a big improvement on the dingy, windowless Newcastle Pub of its former life. This is a good spot for people-watching. ◎ *66 Yi Chun St, Sai Kung • Map G3*

Beach Pub
Overlooking the bay and a 10-minute stroll around the waterfront from Sai Kung Town. The Beach Pub has bands on the weekends and a regular crowd of local Chinese and expatriates. ◎ *Beach Resort Hotel, 1780 Tai Mong Tsai Rd, Sai Kung • Map G3*

Railway Tavern
A welcome little watering hole near the Railway Museum in Tai Po. Just the ticket after a hard day's rural meandering. ◎ *Chik Luk Lane, Tai Wai • Map E2*

Poets
Don't let the name fool you. Loud discussions about the previous night's Premier League soccer matches are more likely than pompous declamations in iambic pentameter. ◎ *G/F 55 Yi Chun St, Sai Kung • Map G3*

The Boozer
Much of Sai Kung's expatriate population can be found around the video juke box or watching sport on flat-screen TVs, while eating food brought in from neighbouring restaurants. ◎ *57 Yi Chun St, Sai Kung • Map G3*

Bacco
For a more sophisticated experience head to Bacco, where you can sample their extensive list of wines by the bottle or the glass. Upstairs is JoJo an Indian restaurant run by the same management team. ◎ *21 Man Nin St, Sai Kung • Map G3*

Regal Riverside Hotel
Two bars are on offer here – one lively and sports-oriented, the other more slinky with a great cocktail menu. Both offer a respite from a hard day's shopping in New Town Plaza. ◎ *34–36 Tai Chung Kiu Rd, Sha Tin • Map E3*

Corner Café
The perfect place to start or end a hike through the country-side surrounding Sai Kung. The delicious coffee and desserts on offer will definitely boost your energy levels. ◎ *120 Man Nin St, Sai Kung • Map G3*

Cru Wine Bar and Grill
This upscale restaurant serves contemporary cuisine with Pan-Asian accents. Prices are a little high but the quality and service are excellent. ◎ *18 Wan King Path, Sai Kung • Map G3*

Hebe One O One
There is a lovely colonial feel to this two-storied, balconied build-ing, painted a soft Mediterranean pink. Upstairs, sea-view tables are perfect for enjoying a drink. ◎ *112 Pak Sha Wan, Sai Kung • Map G3*

Left **Dim sum at Sun Ming Yuen Seafood** Centre and Right **Balcony**

TOP 10 Cheap Eats

1 Pepperoni's
One of the first decent Western-style restaurants in Sai Kung and still going strong. Huge servings, relaxed ambience. Excellent pizza, pasta, nachos, calamari and a good wine selection. ✎ *1592 Po Tung St, Sai Kung • Map G3 • 2791 1738 • $$$*

2 New Tak Kee Seafood Restaurant
Buy your seafood from the market opposite or straight from the boats at the dock and simply pay the restaurant to cook it in your choice of Cantonese style. ✎ *55 See Cheung St, Sai Kung • Map G3 • 2792 0006 • $$*

3 Lardos Steak House
Steaks are cooked to perfection by an owner who supplies Hong Kong's best hotels with their raw material. ✎ *G/F 4B Hang Hau Village, Tseung Kwan O, Sai Kung • Map G3 • 2719 8168 • $$$*

4 Sauce
In an intimate atmosphere, this excellent Italian restaurant serves home-made pasta. It also offers some modern European dishes. ✎ *9 Sha Tsui Path, Sai Kung • Map G3 • 2791 2348 • $$*

5 Sun Ming Yuen Seafood
Excellent-value dim sum and other unpretentious Chinese food is served up in this historic village setting. ✎ *Shop 208 I/F Fanling Centre, 33 San Wan Rd • Map D2 • 2676 1368 • $$*

6 Yau Ley
Fabulous seafood set menus in a little restaurant nestling in Sha Kiu Village, reachable by road, hiking, ferry or boat. ✎ *High Island, Sai Kung • Map G3 • No credit cards • 2791 1822 • www.yauleyseafood.com. hk • $$ (set menu only)*

7 Balcony
Stuff yourself with cut-price pasta at the buffet and marvel at the mediocre service. ✎ *3/F Kowloon Panda Hotel, 3 Tsuen Wah St, Tsuen Wan • Map D3 • 2409 3226 • $$$*

8 AJ's Sri Lankan Cuisine
Light and tasty curries from the Indian Ocean can be enjoyed at Hong Kong's only Sri Lankan restaurant. ✎ *14 Sai Kung Hoi Pong St • Map G3 • 2792 2555 • $$*

9 Honeymoon Dessert (Moon Key)
Good-sized portions of various traditional deserts, with durian eaters segregated so as not to offend others with the strong smell of the fruit. Open until 2am. ✎ *10A–C Po Tung Road, Sai Kung • Map G3 • No credit cards • 2792 4991 • $*

10 Shaffi's Indian
The owner is famous in these parts as the former chef for many years for British and Gurkha troops at Shek Kong barracks. After the Handover, he set up his shop in Yuen Long – where his faithful fans still seek out his top curries. ✎ *14 Fau Tsoi St, Yuen Long • Map C2 • 2476 7885 • $$*

Note: Unless otherwise stated, all restaurants accept credit cards

Price Categories

For a three-course meal for one with half a bottle of wine (or equivalent meal) and extra charges.

$	under HK$100
$$	HK$100–$250
$$$	HK$250–$450
$$$$	HK$450–$600
$$$$$	over HK$600

Royal Park Chinese

🔟 Restaurants

Jaspa's
Good fusion food, friendly staff and lots of antipodean wines at reasonable prices. ◈ *13 Sha Tsui Path, Sai Kung • Map G3 • 2792 6388 • $$$*

Tung Kee Seafood Restaurant
Point at what you want from the huge range of sea creatures swimming in waterfront tanks and haggle a bit. They bag it; you take it to the kitchen; they cook it; you enjoy one of the best seafood meals in Hong Kong. ◈ *9/F, 96–102 Man Nin St, Sai Kung • Map G3 • 2792 7453 • $$$*

Loaf On
Sai Kung's first Michelin-starred restaurant serves authentic Cantonese cuisine. Some locals claim the seafood dishes are the equal of any restaurant in Hong Kong. ◈ *49 Market St, Sai Kung • Map G3 • 2792 9966 • $$$*

Royal Park Chinese
Classy Cantonese cooking – not an easy thing to find in Sha Tin. Specialities include shark's fin soup and crispy chicken. ◈ *2/F Royal Park Hotel, 8 Pak Hok Ting St, Sha Tin • Map E3 • 2694 3968 • $$$*

Ristorante Firenze
Generally packed, and when you try their pastas washed down with well-priced red wines you'll know why. Good pizza too. ◈ *60 Po Tung Rd, Sai Kung • Map G3 • 2792 0898 • $$$*

Sham Tseng Yue Kee Roast Goose Restaurant
Locals can't get enough of the stewed goose intestines, though the less exotic roast goose with salt and pepper is a better bet for tourists. ◈ *9 Sham Tseng San Tsuen, Sham Tseng • Map D3 • 2491 0105 • $$*

Anthony's Catch
The imported seafood cooked Italian-style with home-made pasta and served with Italian wines, has made this one of the most popular restaurants in the area. ◈ *1826B Po Tung Rd, Sai Kungi • Map G3 • 2792 8474 • $$$*

One Thirty-One
Accessible by road or private boat, this restaurant serves food from its own organic farm. Seats only 20, so book ahead. ◈ *131 Tseng Tsau Village, Shap Sze Heung, Sai Kung • Map G3 • 2791 2684 • $$$$$*

Tai Wing Wah
Specializes in dim sum brunches and Poon Choi – a New Territories casserole. ◈ *2–6 On Ning Rd, Yuen Long • Map C2 • 2476 9888 • $$*

Sha Tin 18
In the Sha Tin Hyatt Regency Hotel, this stylish Chinese restaurant is especially good for southern Chinese seafood and meat dishes. There is a large outdoor terrace for alfresco meals. ◈ *18 Chak Cheung St, Sha Tin • Map F3 • 3723 1234 • $$$*

⮊ Following pages Spiral sticks of incense

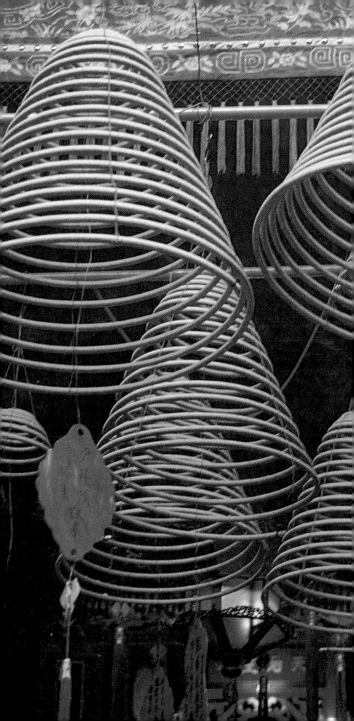

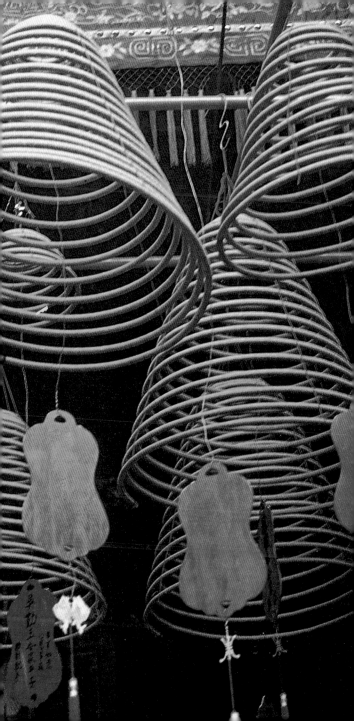

Left **Tai O** Centre **Lamma Island** Right **Lobster**

Outlying Islands

HONG KONG IS THOUGHT OF *as a city not an archipelago, but there are 260 islands in the group and, assuming you can haul yourself out of the downtown bars and boutiques, some of Hong Kong's most sublime experiences await you there. Now that it is connected to the city by bridge, the largest of the islands, Lantau, is losing the quirky languor it once had; but the smaller islands offer plenty of compensations. From the narrow lanes of Cheung Chau to the outdoor raves of Lamma's Power Station Beach, Hong Kong's islands give you many opportunities to lose yourself.*

TOP 10 Sights in the Outlying Islands

1. Lantau – Mui Wo
2. Lantau – Tai O
3. Lantau – Sunset Peak
4. Lantau – Trappist Monastery
5. Lamma – Sok Kwu Wan
6. Lamma – Yung Shue Wan
7. Po Toi
8. Tap Mun
9. Peng Chau
10. Cheung Chau Island

Left **China Bear Pub, Lantau** Right **Sunset Peak, Lantau**

Stilt houses, **Tai O**

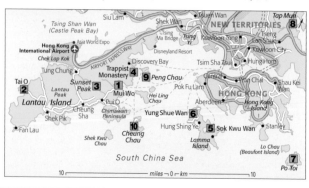

Mui Wo beach, Lantau Island

1 Lantau: Mui Wo

The main ferry from Hong Kong Island to Lantau docks at Mui Wo, or Silvermine Bay as the British named it. It's a good starting point from which to explore the island, though not the most beautiful spot on Lantau. Most of the restaurants and bars and a supermarket are just around the corner from the ferry pier. There is also a beach five minutes' walk to the northeast. Enjoy a beer and a game of snooker or stock up for a picnic before walking or beachcombing. ◎ *Map C5*

2 Lantau: Tai O

Lying on the far western coast of Lantau, the pretty village of Tai O is worth the long haul from downtown Hong Kong. Sitting in a tidal estuary, this is one of the last places in Hong Kong where you can see the traditional stilt housing of southern Chinese fishing villages. Some are as small as dolls' houses. For an authentic Hong Kong consumable, buy a jar of shrimp paste, a powerful type of fish sauce created by fermenting shrimp and spices in a barrel in the sun. It's actually much better than it sounds. ◎ *Map A5*

3 Lantau: Sunset Peak

For the reasonably fit, Sunset Peak offers the finest views on Lantau. The 934-m (3,063-ft) high mountain, Hong Kong's second highest, commands great views across Hong Kong, down onto the international airport, Po Lin Monastery and the lovely wooded valleys of this sparsely inhabited terrain. Hardy souls stay at the nearby Youth Hostel and head up the peak for Hong Kong's most spectacular sunrise. Obviously all this only applies in clear conditions. ◎ *Map B5*

4 Lantau: Trappist Monastery

The chapel, next to a dilapidated old dairy farm, is open to visitors willing to observe the silence of the monastery. Apart from that, there's not much to see at the monastery itself, but it's a good excuse for a gentle woodland walk to or from Discovery Bay. The monastery is also served by a ferry pier with infrequent Kaido services to Discovery Bay and the island of Peng Chau *(see p115)*, which has many seafood restaurants. ◎ *Map C5 • Free*

Tai O fishing village

For Lantau's Big Buddha and Po Lin Monastery **See pp28–9**

113

Peng Chau harbour

Lamma: Sok Kwu Wan

Don't expect many sights in Lamma's main area of development on the east coast. Sok Kwu Wan is known mainly for its quarry and wall-to-wall seafood restaurants along the harbour front. The seafood tanks are a sight in themselves, however, with some monster-sized fish and crustaceans. There's not much to differentiate most restaurants, although the standard is generally very good. Have a look at the pretty Tin Hau Temple at the end of the main street. The lovely 3-mile (5-km) circular walk to the sleepy, remote village and beach at Yung Shue Ha is recommended for the reasonably fit. ◈ Map E6 • Regular ferries from Hong Kong Island

Lamma: Yung Shue Wan

Lamma's western coast also has a harbour, with lots of bars and eating choices along the village's endearingly ramshackle main street. Watch villagers, resident expats and fellow visitors wander by, before hitting the well-kept beach at Hung

Lantau's Pink Dolphins

The rare and endangered dolphins of the Pearl River Delta can usually be found at play near the coast of Lantau. A guided boat trip to see them is certainly worthwhile. Learn about the lives of these creatures and the threats they face, including pollution, overfishing and lethal boat propellers and hydrofoils. Tours leave at least four times a week (see pp54 & 145).

Shing Ye, a 20-minute walk to the southwest. ◈ Map D5 • Regular ferries from Hong Kong Island

Po Toi

Getting to this craggy, barely inhabited outcrop of rock south of Hong Kong Island is most easily accomplished by taking the ferries that run from Stanley and Aberdeen. It's worth the effort for the secluded walks and spectacular cliff views over the South China Sea. Round off your day with a meal at the island's only restaurant, the Ming Kee (see p117). ◈ Map F6 • Ferry from Stanley or Aberdeen Tue, Thu, Sat, Sun & public hols

Left **Drying fish** Right **Beach at Hung Shing Ye, Lamma**

Fishermen

Tap Mun

To the north of the Sai Kung Peninsula, tiny Tap Mun, also known as "grass island", is another remote destination with only a couple of daily connections with the mainland. The rewards are striking rock formations, pounding seas, a herd of cattle and relative seclusion. The island's Tin Hau Temple is surprisingly large and beautiful. Take a picnic, as there are few eating opportunities. Nor is there any accommodation on the island, so be sure to catch that last ferry. ◎ *Map H2 • Ferries from Wong Shek and Ma Liu Shui*

Peng Chau

This tiny island nestling off the coast of Lantau, opposite Discovery Bay, remains in many ways a traditional Hong Kong coastal community. You wander among its narrow alleys, tiny shops and temples to the gentle soundtrack of a distant game of mahjong or the sound of Cantonese opera leaking from an old radio set. But there's no beach, and few eating choices, although the seafood is cheap. ◎ *Map C5 • Ferries from Hong Kong Island and Lantau's Discovery Bay*

Cheung Chau Island

This former pirate haven retains much of its traditional character, from the small-scale shipyards at the harbour's edge to the old temples and shrines that dot its narrow alleys. With many of its inhabitants still being fishermen, it's a good destination for cheap seafood. There are also a couple of excellent beaches *(see pp24–5)*.

A Day on Lantau

Morning

🕐 Make a reasonably early start for Lantau from the outlying islands ferry terminal on Hong Kong Island. After disembarking at **Mui Wo** *(see p113)*, take the No.1 bus from outside the ferry pier to the old fishing village of **Tai O** *(see p113)* on the far northwestern coast.

Take in the sights and smells of this ancient settlement before catching bus 21 to Ngong Ping for the **Big Buddha and Po Lin Monastery**, or take a ride in the Ngong Ping 360 Cable Car *(see pp28–9)*.

🍴 Have a vegetarian lunch at the monastery, or take a picnic: The area around Ngong Ping is great for gentle rambles with a view and some serious hill climbing (Lantau Peak).

Afternoon

If time still permits, take the bus back towards Mui Wo, but jump out at the fantastic, clean and usually deserted beach at Cheung Sha (ask the driver to let you know when). Spend a relaxed afternoon paddling, swimming and sunbathing on this glorious stretch of golden sand.

Slake your afternoon thirst and tea-time hunger at **The Stoep** *(see p117)*, which offers Mediterranean-style and South African food.

From here it's a short ride back into Mui Wo. Before catching the return ferry, squeeze in a drink at the Hippo or **China Bear** *(see p117)*, two convivial bars near the ferry pier.

Left **Big Buddha** Centre **Boats, Lantau** Right **Hakka woman**

🔟 Photo Opportunities

Big Buddha on Lantau
The dramatic setting in itself is worth a picture, let alone the mighty Buddha (see pp28–9).

Any Ferry Aft Deck
Gain some perspective on the dramatic skyline of the islands. The Star Ferries offer the best chance to capture the dramatic skyscrapers (see pp14–15).

Hatted Hakka Women
The large woven hats draped with a black cotton fringe come from the Hakka people, once a distinct ethnic group in the region. Many women wear these hats around Hong Kong, though not all wearers are ethnic Hakka.

Cheung Chau Harbour
Handsome high-prowed fishing boats, squat sampans and busy boatyards are just some of the sights (see pp24–5).

Tai O Village, Lantau
The old fishing village on the remote northwest coast is the last settlement in the territory with a significant number of stilt houses, some almost as small as play houses (see p113).

Ngong Ping 360 Cable Car
The 25-minute cable car ride provides one of the best photo opportunities in Hong Kong. From the car, you can see out over Lantau North Country Park, the South China Sea, Hong Kong International Airport, the Tung Chung Valley and the rest of the surrounding area (see p55).

Lamma Restaurants' Seafood Tanks
The restaurants display the subject of their menus live and swimming in huge outdoor fish tanks. You'll see some edible leviathans here from monster grouper to giant lobsters and an absorbing array of other fidgeting crustacea and teeming sealife.

View of Airport from Lantau Peak
Take a powerful lens on a clear day to get decent shots of the airport from Lantau Peak. The summit also offers terrific views down onto the monastery and surrounding country. ◈ Map B5

Hong Kong Airport Planespotters Platform
There's no official viewing area at the airport, so take a taxi or walk to the small hill (the only natural part of this man-made island) just opposite Tung Chung town. There's a footpath to the summit and its pagoda. ◈ Map B5

Tsing Ma Bridge Lookout Point
If big construction projects move the earth for you, then head to the free Airport Core Programme Exhibition Centre in Ting Kau. The viewing platform on the roof offers a great opportunity to photograph the elegant Tsing Ma and Ting Kau bridges. ◈ Map D3

China Bear

Price Categories

For a three-course meal for one with half a bottle of wine (or equivalent meal) and extra charges.

$	under HK$100
$$	HK$100–$250
$$$	HK$250–$450
$$$$	HK$450–$600
$$$$$	over HK$600

TOP 10 Places to Eat and Drink

China Bear, Lantau
Missed the ferry? Never mind. Nip round the corner for one of the cheap lunch specials and 30 kinds of bottled and draft beer. ✆ G/F, Mui Wo Centre • Map C5 • 2984 7360 • No credit cards • $$

The Stoep, Lantau
Good Mediterranean and South African fodder are served up on one of Lantau's loveliest beaches. Try the platters or the cold Cape-style curried fish. ✆ 32 Lower Cheung Sha Village • Map B6 • 2980 2699 • $$

McSorley's Ale House, Lantau
Popular with home-sick expats craving the taste of home, dishes include fish and chips, pies, curries and hearty Sunday roasts. There's also Guinness and a choice of real ales. ✆ Block B, DB Plaza, Discovery Bay • Map C4 • 2987 8280 • $$$

Cheung Chau Windsurfing Centre Bistro, Cheung Chau
The "all-day" breakfast, snacks and mainly Western entrées are good enough to keep you from exercise altogether. Open 1–6pm. ✆ 1 Hai Pak Rd, Cheung Chau • Map C6 • 2981 8316 • $$

Rainbow Seafood, Lamma
One of Lamma's better places for a full seafood splurge with a harbour view. The locals love it, and so will you. ✆ 16–20 First Street, Sok Kwu Wan • Map E6 • 2982 8100 • $$

Tin Yin Dessert, Cheung Chau
Waterside canteen serving refreshing and unusual treats – try the sago with jelly and coconut milk. ✆ 9 Tai Hing Tai Rd • Map C6 • No credit cards • $

Bookworm Café, Lamma
This place wears its ethical, veggie heart on its sleeve, with its twee slogans to peace, love and tofu on its walls. Don't be put off. Service is friendly; the fresh food and juices exceptional. ✆ 79 Yung Shue Wan Main Street • Map D5 • 2982 4838 • No credit cards • $$

Lamma Man Fung Seafood, Lamma
Neither the best nor the cheapest seafood on Lamma, but the setting of this restaurant – overlooking the bay – is superb. ✆ 5 Main St, Yung Shue Wan • Map D5 • 2982 0719 • $$

Cheung Kee, Cheung Chau
Somewhat shabby premises, but the noodles are fresh and the dumplings and wontons are just right. There's no signage in English but it's easy to find, just by the ferry pier. ✆ 83 Praya St • Map C6 • 2981 8078 • No credit cards • $

Ming Kee Seafood, Po Toi
Run by a restaurateur and his seven daughters, this is Po Toi's best restaurant. Reach it by junk or from Stanley on a Sunday (see p114). ✆ Tai Wan • Map F6 • 2849 7038 • No credit cards • $$

Note: Unless otherwise stated, all restaurants accept credit cards

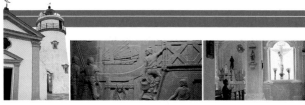

Left **Guia Lighthouse** Centre **Relief, Maritime Museum** Right **São Domingos**

Macau

GAMBLING IS INDISPUTABLY MACAU'S MAIN SCENE – *it claims to earn more revenue from its 30-odd casinos than Las Vegas* – *catering mainly to weekend visitors from Hong Kong and, increasingly, mainland China. However, the Portuguese also had 400 years of rich history here, leaving behind whole districts of cobbled lanes and impressive Iberian architecture. The indigenous cuisine, which fuses together Chinese and Portuguese elements, is another draw.*

🔟 Sights in Macau

1. Avenida da Republica
2. Guia Lighthouse
3. Ruinas do São Paulo
4. Largo do Senado
5. Cultural Centre
6. Protestant Cemetery
7. Camões Grotto
8. Forteleza do Monte
9. Dom Pedro Theatre
10. St Joseph's Seminary

Lou Lim leoc Garden

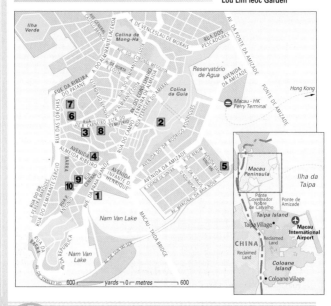

Ruinas de São Paulo

Avenida da Republica

The graceful boughs of banyan trees stretch over this elegant avenue, shading the candy-coloured pageant of colonial-era architecture. Unlike in Hong Kong, many of Macau's historic piles survive in excellent condition. At the gorgeous fort-turned-hotel of Pousada de São Tiago, the road becomes Rua de S. Tiago da Barra; follow it around the point to find yourself between the A-ma Temple and the Maritime Museum (see p122).

Guia Lighthouse

This most visible of Macau's landmarks has kept its lonely vigil on Guia Hill since 1638, its flashing beacon beckoning to everyone from Portuguese traders to ferocious pirates and marauding Dutch navy boats. Catch the cable car up the hill, take in the 360-degree panorama from Macau's highest point and enjoy a leisurely stroll back down. ⊗ Free

Ruinas do São Paulo

The façade and intricate mosaic floor are all that remain of Macau's grandest church, perched atop a steep flight of stone steps and propped up by a viewing platform at the rear. In its heyday, the Jesuit-designed Cathedral was hailed as the greatest monument to Christianity in the East. It caught fire during a massive typhoon in 1835, and only extensive structural work in the early 1990s stopped the façade from crumbling to rubble. ⊗ Museum of Sacred Art 9am–6pm • Free

Largo do Senado

Brightly painted colonial buildings and slightly psychedelic paving makes this square in the heart of Macau a favourite with photographers. At one end sits the Leal Senado, or Loyal Senate, now the seat of the municipal government but once the Portuguese headquarters. It was thus named because Macau refused to recognise the 17th-century Spanish occupation of Portugal. ⊗ Leal Senado 9am–9pm • Closed Mon • Free

Left **Food stalls** Right **Largo do Senado**

For entry requirements to Macau See p136

Left **Camões Grotto** Right **Interior of St Joseph's Seminary**

Cultural Centre

5 This elegant building was designed and put up in time for the December 1999 Handover to China. In fact, the actual ceremony took place behind the centre in a temporary structure designed to look like a giant Chinese lantern. The centre is the focal point for the Macau Arts Festival each March. The only mystery is why there is what appears to be a ski-jump on the roof. ◈ *11am–7pm daily • Free*

Headstone

Protestant Cemetery

6 More interesting than it sounds – indeed, you might find yourself spending hours wandering this grave-dotted grove, reading inscriptions to plague-doomed sailors and colonial adventurers. Those at rest include painter George Chinnery (the Mandarin Oriental's bar in Hong Kong is named after him) and Robert Morrison, the first Protestant to venture to China in search of converts. ◈ *9am–5:30pm daily • Free*

Camões Grotto

7 The author of the 16th-century Portuguese epic *The Lusiads* may never actually have visited Macau, but don't try telling the local Portuguese. Luis Vaz de Camões specialized in overblown,

patriotic verse – a bust of him peers through the grotto's gloom. The adjoining gardens are popular with old men and their caged birds first thing in the morning. ◈ *6am–10pm • Free*

Fortaleza do Monte

8 These walls bounded the original Portuguese settlement in

Fortaleza do Monte

Colonial-style buildings

Macau, a well-stocked fort, which its inhabitants boasted could withstand years of siege. The sternest test came in 1622 when the Dutch, who had been coveting Macau for years, made their move, only to be decisively beaten. The Portuguese military were based here up until 1966, at which point Portugal decided it was more politic to be administrators of Macau rather than gun-toting colonialists. ✎ *7am–7pm daily • Free*

Dom Pedro Theatre

The first Western-style lyric theatre in the East, the Dom Pedro opened in 1858 designed in a Neo-Classical style. It is still used to host plays and performances. The hike up the hill is worth it for a look at a piece of theatrical history. ✎ *9am–6pm • Macau Tourism Office for performance details • 8399 6699*

St Joseph's Seminary

The Jesuits constructed this ornate lemon-yellow chapel between 1746 and 1758, modelled on the Bon Gesu Basilica in Rome. Its original dedication plaque namechecks Portuguese King João V, Macau Bishop Hilario de St Rosa and Chinese Qing-dynasty Emperor Qian Long. The original bells still ring out each day, and all sorts of fascinating Catholic artifacts can be found within.

A Day in Macau

Morning

Catch a taxi to the **Ruinas de São Paulo** *(see p119)* in the heart of Macau, pose for a picture on the steps in front, then lose yourself in the surrounding streets full of Chinese and antique furniture shops. The rich red lacquered trunks and cabinets, old teak tables and chairs are all cheaper than in Hong Kong's antique stores.

When your feet start to protest, take a cab across the causeways to Coloane Island and a sangria-soaked lunch at **Fernando's** *(see p125)*. Get a large jug of piquant Sangria in, then go for the fried chicken, garlic prawns, clams and sardines. The bread is hot and moreish, and the Portuguese salad is simplistic bliss.

After Lunch

Walk off lunch on **Hac Sa Beach** *(see p122)* or wobble your way to the minibus outside Fernando's and travel to Taipa village, which has picturesque houses and shops.

Then grab another taxi and head to the **Macau Tower** *(see p122)* for magnificent views of Macau and across the sea to Taipa, Coloane and the Cotai Strip. If you're feeling adventurous, you could try the Skywalk around the outer rim or even the bungee jump from the Observation Deck.

If you have the stamina, make your way to Avenida Dr Sun Yat Sen and its many bars for a night on the tiles or head to the swish bars and casinos of the Cotai Strip *(see p123)*.

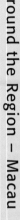

Left **Lou Lim Ieoc Garden** Centre **Rua da Felicidade** Right **Maritime Museum**

🔟 Best of the Rest

Macau Tower
Often dubbed "Dr Ho's erection" after casino mogul Dr Stanley Ho. At 338 m (1,107 ft), the tower pips the Eiffel Tower and forms the centre of a convention and restaurant complex. The Skywalk and the glass-floored revolving restaurant are not for the faint of heart. ◈ *Nam Van Lakes area*

Pousada de Coloane
Macau's first beachfront hotel is a top spot for a few cold drinks when the sun is shining. ◈ *Cheoc Van Praia, Coloane • 2888 2143*

Lou Lim Ieoc Garden
Shady trees, lots of benches, lotus ponds. ◈ *Avenida do Conselheiro Ferreira De Almeida • 6am–6pm daily*

Macau Museum
Good displays on history and architecture. ◈ *Citadel of São Paolo do Monte • 2835 7911 • 10am– 6pm. Closed Mon • Adm*

São Domingos
The pale yellow Spanish-style church towers over the Largo do Senado square. White ants forced extensive renovations in the mid-1990s. More than 300 sacred works of art are in the adjoining museum. ◈ *Largo do Domingos • 10am–6pm daily • Free*

A-ma Temple
Images of junks decorate this pretty collection of halls dedicated to the patron deity of sailors, after whom the name "Macau" is derived. ◈ *Rua do Almirante Sergio • 8am–7pm daily • Free*

Rua da Felicidade
The "street of happiness" once teemed with brothels, hence its somewhat ironically bestowed name. It's now a quaint, cobbled thoroughfare full of cheap eateries.

Maritime Museum
The place to head if you are interested in Macau's colourful seagoing past. ◈ *Largo do Pagode da Barra • 2859 5481 • 10am–5:30pm. Closed Tue • Adm*

Pousada de São Tiago
The beautiful hotel *(see p154)* overlooking the bay began life in the 17th century as a Portuguese fort hewn from the rock.
◈ *Avenida da República • 2837 8111*

Hac Sa Beach
Black mineral sand beach. Enjoy a stroll around the headland to the Westin Resort *(see p154)* for a drink. ◈ *Coloane*

Left **Wynn** Centre **The Venetian** Right **Sands**

TOP10 Places to Gamble

1 Grand Lisboa
When casino mogul Dr Stanley Ho's original Lisboa hotel began to look dowdy, he built this extravagant party palace complete with giant casino and 15 restaurants next door. Nowhere says "Macau bling" quite like this place.◉ *Avenida de Lisboa • 2828 3838 • 24 hours*

2 Macau Jockey Club
A bit more down-at-heel than its high-tech, cashed-up Hong Kong counterpart.
◉ *Estrada Gov Albano da Oliveira, Taipa • 2882 0868 • Race meetings Wed or Thu & weekends • Adm*

3 Canidrome
Go the dishlickers! This is the only greyhound racing club in Asia. ◉ *Avenida General Castelo Branco • 2833 3399 • Tue, Thu & weekends • Adm*

4 City of Dreams
This opulent mega-casino is aimed at punters with a penchant for ostentatious interiors and deluxe facilities. ◉ *Estrada de Istmo, Cotai Strip • 8868 6688 • 24 hours*

5 Sands Cotai Central
This resort combines 3 hotels, 20 dining options, shopping and gambling on a vast scale.
◉ *Estrada da Baía de N Senhora da Esperança • 8805 8888 • 24 hrs*

6 The Venetian
The full Las Vegas experience has been transported to the tropics. Live shows and big-brand shopping provide a welcome break from gambling. ◉ *Estrada da Baía de N Senhora da Esperança, Cotai Strip • 2882 8888 • 24 hours*

7 MGM Grand
An astonishing rippling façade, a lavish spa and a vast gambling hall in the style of a Portuguese town square can be found at MGM Grand. ◉ *Avenida Dr Sun Yat Sen, NAPE • 8802 8888 • 24 hours*

8 Wynn
This is one of the most lavish casinos in Macau. The interior is decked out with floral carpets, extravagant chandeliers and plenty of colour. ◉ *Rua Cidade de Sintra, NAPE • 2888 9966 • 24 hours*

9 Kam Pek Casino
The loyal clientele of local punters here can be rude to tourists and flashy Hong Kongers. Prolonged eye contact with habitués is inadvisable. ◉ *Rua de Foshan • 24 hours*

10 Sands
The first of the Vegas-style, mega-casinos to arrive on the waterfront.
◉ *Largo de Monte Carlo 203 • 2888 3388 • 24 hours*

Left **Oskar's Bar** Centre **Vasco** Right **Casablanca Café**

TOP 10 Cafés, Bars and Clubs

Bellini Lounge
Tucked in a corner of the Venetian is this stylish bar. The surroundings may be plush, but the emphasis is on good live music, either from the two house bands, or from special guests. Check with the front desk for details of who is performing. ⊗ *Venetian Hotel, Estrada da Baía de North Senhora da Esperança, Cotai Strip*

Vida Rica Bar
Great for watching Macau's movers and shakers, this extravagantly styled bar has an arty interior and fabulous harbour views. ⊗ *Mandarin Oriental Macau, Avenida Dr Sun Yat Sen*

Club CUBIC
Rather fabulous Hong Kong-owned club, with live DJs and cocktails at the weekend. A good place for celebrity-spotting. ⊗ *Level 2, City of Dreams, Cotai*

360 Café
This revolving bar, restaurant and café at the top of the Macau Tower boasts peerless views over the old city, the sea and islands. ⊗ *60/F Macau Tower, Lago San Vai*

Oskar's Bar
A mix of tourists and locals gather at this typical hotel-style bar, as well as the odd exponent of the world's oldest profession. ⊗ *G/F Holiday Inn Hotel, Rua de Pequim*

Vasco
Enjoy tasty tapas-style fare and imaginative cocktails at Vasco. Live music at night. ⊗ *G/F Grand Lapa Hotel, Avenida da Amidaze*

Talker Pub
Feisty locals at play, so tread carefully. There's always football on the television and cheap beer. ⊗ *104 Rua de Pedro Coutinho*

D2
This two-storey dance club features pop, rock, house and techno, with bar-top pole dancers at weekends. ⊗ *2/F, AIA Tower, 251A–301 Avenida Comercial de Macau*

Flame Bar
A fine selection of cocktails and an irrepressibly upscale party vibe feature at this lounge and club. Great fun if your credit card is up to it. ⊗ *Level 2, Hard Rock Hotel, City of Dreams, Cotai*

Casablanca Café
There's a pool table, lots of red velvet and posters recalling the famous film. Enjoy the in-house music but resist the temptation to say "play it again, Sam" to the surly staff. ⊗ *Av. Dr Sun Yat Sen*

Price Categories

For a three-course meal for one with half a bottle of wine (or equivalent meal) and extra charges.

$	under HK$100
$$	HK$100–$250
$$$	HK$250–$450
$$$$	HK$450–$600
$$$$$	over HK$600

Left **Grilled sardines, Fernando's** Right **Clube Militar de Macau**

🔟 Places to Eat

Fernando's
Still unspoiled by its far-flung fame, this is the perfect place for a long, lazy liquid lunch. Succulent roast chicken, grilled sardines, killer sangria and garlic prawns to die for. ◈ *Praia Hac Sa 9, Coloane • 2888 2264 (booking rec) • No credit cards • $$$*

A Lorcha
A fine proponent of Macanese cooking, which blends the cuisines of East and West. Try spicy grilled African chicken, *bacalhau* (baked codfish) and *caldo verde* (potato purée soup). ◈ *Rua do Almirante Sergio 289 • 2831 3193 • $$$*

Litoral
The best Macanese restaurant in town – try the curried crab or stuffed prawns. ◈ *Rua do Almirante Sergio 261 • 2896 7878 • $$$*

Solmar
An old favourite among locals. Try the rich seafood soup with chunks of codfish that melt in your mouth. ◈ *Avenida da Praia Grande 512 • 2896 7878 • $$$*

Ou Mun
The best place in town for heart-starting morning coffee and pastries. ◈ *12 Travesa de Sao Domingos • 2837 2207 • No credit cards • $$*

Robuchon au Dôme
This exquisite fine-dining parlour boasts not only three Michelin stars but superlative city views. ◈ *43/F Grand Lisboa Hotel, Avenida de Lisboa • 8803 7878 • $$$$$*

Clube Militar de Macau
Built to cater for army bigwigs, the Military Club is one of the best examples of classical European architecture in Asia. Gourmet Portuguese cuisine. ◈ *Avenida da Praia Grande 975 • 2871 4000 • $$$$*

Espaco Lisboa
Tucked away in a Coloane village and presided over by the Portuguese chef-owner, this rustic restaurant is a reminder of sleepy, pre-development Macao. ◈ *Rua das Gaivotas 8, Coloane • 2888 2226 • $$$*

Tim's Kitchen
With one Michelin star, this Cantonese restaurant is less flashy than some of the glitzy ones in town but its signature seafood dishes are highly regarded. ◈ *Hotel Lisboa, 2–4 Avenida de Lisboa • 8803 3682 • $$$$*

The Eight
Enjoy superb Chinese food at this modern, lavish restaurant with two Michelin stars. ◈ *2/F Grand Lisboa Hotel, Avenida de Lisboa • 8803 7788 • $$$$$*

Note: Unless otherwise stated, all restaurants accept credit cards

Left **Crabs, Dong Men food market** Left **Minsk World** Right **Splendid China theme park**

Shenzhen

ITHIN LIVING MEMORY, *Shenzhen, just across the New Territories border, was a minor township in communist China, its communal fisheries set in extraordinary juxtaposition to capitalist Hong Kong. Yet Shenzhen (or "Shumchun") has gone from gulag to Gotham City in the space of 20 years. The reason is its status as a free-trading Special Economic Zone, which has created wealth and allured schemers, tricksters and beggars from all over China. To them, Shenzhen is an ersatz Hong Kong; to the visitor, Shenzhen's tawdry commercialism offers a glimpse of the brave new China. Enjoyable, assuming you maintain a stiff sense of irony.*

Sights

1. Luo Hu Commercial City
2. Dong Men District
3. Minsk World
4. China Folk Culture Village
5. Splendid China
6. Window of the World
7. Happy Valley
8. Mission Hills Golf Club
9. Bargain Beauty Treatments
10. Honey Lake Resort

Luo Hu Commercial City

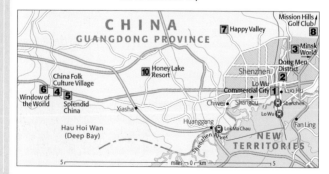

1 Luo Hu Commercial City

Right by the border station, this large mall is the most convenient place to shop in Shenzhen. Inside its teeming five stories are virtually all the consumer goods you could ever desire, in exhaustive and exhausting quantities. The brands are either Chinese (often of solid build) or fake Western (take your chances). Countless stalls sell all manner of clothes, footwear, jewellery, watches, accessories and electronic goods. A huge textiles market is on the fifth floor. Expect to haggle over prices: offer no more than 10 per cent of the first asking price to start with. ◎ By border stn

Minsk World

2 Dong Men District

If you have the energy to tackle it, a vast expanse of clothes shops awaits you in the sprawling Dong Men district. Remember that clothes such as men's shirts will be cut for the Asian figure, so try before buying. At the eastern edge of Dong Men is a footbridge leading to another huge fabric market, located above a food market. There is no English signposting here, though, so be sure to have the destination written down in Chinese. ◎ Dong Men district, a couple of miles N of Luo Hu

3 Minsk World

The ironies come thick and fast aboard this former Soviet aircraft carrier, selling American hot dogs from its flight deck. It's a hugely popular destination for Chinese tourists, though few Westerners visit. Here you can thrill at footage of missiles exploding in fireballs of increasing magnitude set against a spaghetti western soundtrack; behold stuffed Russian space dog Strelka; and applaud a baffling Russian cabaret act. ◎ Yantian district • 2535 5333 • 9:30am–6:30pm daily • Adm

4 China Folk Culture Village

Full-size recreations of traditional villages are peopled by well groomed, eternally happy folk representing different ethnic Chinese groups. An anthropologist's nightmare perhaps, but it will give you some idea of China's diverse cultural and ethnic melting pot. ◎ Overseas Chinese Town • 2660 0626 • 9am–9:30pm daily • Adm

5 Splendid China

The architectural wonders of China, including recreations of Beijing's Imperial Palace, the Terracotta Warriors of Xi'an and the Great Wall are on show here. ◎ Overseas Chinese Town • 2660 0626 • 9am–6pm daily • Adm

Splendid China

For mainland China visa information See p136

127

Left **Splendid China** Right **Window of the World**

Window of the World

Of all the oddities springing from Shenzhen's fevered theme parks appetite, Window of the World is, to Western eyes, the most surreal: a reduction (literally and metaphorically) of the real world. Mount Fuji becomes a 6-m (20-ft) slagheap, tourists pose in Thai national dress in front of the Taj Mahal and, poignantly, Manhattan retains its World Trade Center. Live shows are put on at set times on most "continents", including one from a suspiciously Asiatic-looking African tribe. There's also a Grand Canyon flume ride and a real snow ski-slope.
⊛ Overseas Chinese Town • 2660 8000
• 9am–10:30pm daily • Adm

Happy Valley

This theme park gives Hong Kong's Ocean Park a run for its money, with the bonus of a tidal pool, adrenalin-inducing rides such as the Space Shot, an assault course and martial arts demon-strations. Use the Happy Line monorail to travel between this and other nearby theme parks. ⊛ Overseas Chinese Town • 2694 9168
• 9:30am–10pm Mon–Fri, 9am–10pm Sat, Sun • Adm

Mission Hills Golf Club

Many Hong Kong executives come across the border to play at this five-star,

216-hole golf club. Alternatively, you can play tennis on one of the resort's 51 courts. ⊛ Mission Hills Rd, Guanlan town • Reservations 2802 0888 • Shuttle bus from HK's Lok Ma Chau every 20 mins • www.mission hillschina.com

Bargain Beauty Treatments

When you reach breaking point with all the shopping malls and theme parks, rest and refresh yourself with an exceptionally cheap foot or back massage, or perhaps some nail painting. A vast range of treatments are available at Luo Hu (see p127). Hotel health centres offer the assurance of professional reflexology and traditional massage as well as the opportunity to be pampered.

Honey Lake Resort

Almost every kind of leisure facility is on the city's doorstep at Honey Lake, including a large amusement park, shopping mall, golf courses and indoor and outdoor pools. ⊛ Shennan Rd, Futian district • 2989 7388 • Adm

Mission Hills Golf Club

Price Categories

For a three-course meal for one with half a bottle of wine (or equivalent meal) and extra charges.

$	under HK$100
$$	HK$100–$250
$$$	HK$250–$450
$$$$	HK$450–$600
$$$$$	over HK$600

Laurel Restaurant

🔟 Places to Eat and Drink

1 Laurel Restaurant
Terrific classic Cantonese restaurant that is packed all day but worth a wait. 🔍 *Shop 5010, 5/F Luo Hu Commercial City • 8232 3668 • $$*

2 Jingyi Chaguan
Elegant vegetarian teahouse restaurant that attracts Buddhist monks as well as resident foreigners. Try the dim sum. 🔍 *7/F, Jingtang Dasha, 3038 Bao'an Nan Lu, Luohu • 2558 6555 • No credit cards • $$*

3 Golden Peninsula Chiu Chow
A central location that's easy to find, a clear English menu and polite staff all make this one of the best Chinese restaurants in town. 🔍 *Block B, 1/F Lido Hotel, Dong Men Nan Lu, Luohu • No credit cards • 8225 9988 • $$$*

4 360°
With great night views of Shenzhen, the revolving restaurant atop the luxury Shangri-La Hotel *(see p148)* has an international buffet, hotpots and grills. 🔍 *Shangri-La Hotel, Jianshe Lu • 8396 1380 • $$$*

5 Big Grey Wolf
Highly unusual decor based on the architecture of Gansu, and some tasty Gansu-style lamb and potato dishes. 🔍 *Huafu Lu 1022, Futian • 8324 1818 • No credit cards • $$*

6 Nanyuan Lu
Like most major cities in China, Shenzhen has an active Muslim community. This row of restaurants serves up delicious mutton kebabs, pilau rice and naan breads to hungry tourists and locals alike. 🔍 *Nanyuan Lu, Futian • $$*

7 Xingli
The Chinese restaurant at the swanky Ritz-Carlton Hotel offers delicate Chiu Chow cuisine, originating from the Chaoshan region of China, as well as a selection of Cantonese and Schezuan dishes. 🔍 *116 Fuhua San Rd, Futian • 2222 2222 • $$$$*

8 Casablanca
French- and Italian-influenced food in Shekou district, which is Shenzhen's expat, harbourside bolthole. 🔍 *Seaworld Plaza, Hai Bin Building, Shekou • 2667 6968 • $$*

9 True Colors Dong Men
A quiet Western restaurant with live jazz, great food and English-speaking waiters. 🔍 *4/F Dong Men Friendship City, Jie Fang Lu • 8230 1833 • $$*

360° at the Shangri-La Hotel

🔟 Soho Restaurant and Nightclub
The staff have worked hard on everything from the food to the design in this flashy establishment. 🔍 *Bitao Club, Tai Zi Lu, Shekou • 2669 0148 • $$*

Left **Street scene** Centre **Martial arts in the park** Right **White Swan Hotel, Shamian Island**

Guangzhou

CHINA'S TWO GREAT REVOLUTIONS, *republican and communist, were born in Guangzhou, which indicates the temperament of this sprawling southern Chinese capital. Far distant from Beijing, the city has gone its own wilful way, and there is still the insouciance of a people who answer to no one. The modern city is at the mercy of miasmic smog and yammering traffic, but it also has enormous personality, from the soaring Canton Tower with the world's highest Ferris wheel to the Han dynasty tombs, plentiful temples, and the charm of Shamian Island's faded 19th-century terraces.*

🔟 Sights in Guangzhou

1. Shamian Island
2. Wandering Among the Gei
3. Hua Lin Temple and Jade Market
4. Chen Clan Temple
5. Temples of Filial Piety and Six Banyan Trees
6. Nanyue Tomb
7. Yuexiu Park
8. White Cloud Mountain
9. Guangdong Museum of Art
10. River Trips

Pagoda at Six Banyan Trees

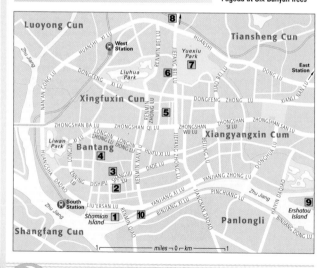

Left **Wandering among the *gei*** Right **Chen Clan Temple**

Shamian Island
The small islet in southwest Guangzhou long served as the main gateway to China, the only place where merchants and diplomats were allowed to do business with the Empire. Today it's a lovely leafy haven, well restored and beautified with some good accommodation, dining and drinking options and quiet riverside walks.

Wandering Among the Gei
Perhaps the simplest yet most worthwhile thing to do in Guangzhou is to wander aimlessly along its *gei*, the narrow alleys between the ancient ramshackle houses in the older parts of town. The streets above Shamian Island up as far as Liwanhu district are especially good. Strolling down these byways gives a sense of the everyday life that has carried on here for hundreds of years. Absorb yourself in the minutiae of domestic life and small-scale

Jade market

industries, such as beauty treatments, maybe in the form of eyebrow plucking with a simple piece of cotton.

Hua Lin Temple and Jade Market
An extensive jade market surrounds the small Buddhist temple of Hua Lin, which is also worth a quick visit. The jade on sale is cheaper than in Hong Kong, although you'll need to be an expert to separate the rare real jade from the fake. Several antique stores and jade and amber sellers can be found west of Kangwang Zhong Lu, and north of Changshang Xi Lu. ⊗ *North of Xiajiu Lu, east of Wen Nan Wen Lu*

Chen Clan Temple
With Chen being the most common family name in the area, it's no surprise that the many groupings of local Chens built a suitably vast temple complex in the 1890s. It's particularly worth a look if you haven't visited any of the ancestral halls in the New Territories of Hong Kong. The most impressive feature is the ornate ceramic friezes adorning the roof, depicting Confucian moral tales. There are also displays (some of admittedly patchy quality) of jade, bone and other local crafts, some for sale. Head to the leafy courtyards for peace and shade. ⊗ *Zhongshan Qi Lu, metro Chen Jia Ci • 8:30am–5pm daily • Adm*

For mainland China visa information **See p136**

Left **Temple of the Six Banyan Trees** Right **Yuexiu Park**

Temples of Filial Piety and Six Banyan Trees

The Temple of Filial Piety (Guang-xiao Si) was a royal temple as far back as the 2nd century BC, and is thought to have served as a Buddhist shrine since the 4th century AD. However, the buildings that stand today were built in the 17th century. It's a lovely place to come and sit beneath venerable, ancient fig trees in quiet courtyards. The nearby Temple of the Six Banyan Trees (Liurong Si) has the oldest and largest pagoda in Guangzhou, standing at 55 m (180 ft), though the banyan trees have sadly died. Ⓢ *Guangxiao Lu*

Nanyue Tomb

A well-presented museum preserves the burial tomb and artifacts of one of the kings of the Southern Yue, who ruled the area in the 2nd century BC. Well signposted in Chinese and English, the tomb offers a glimpse of a culturally sophisticated society. Fine ceramic pillows and some exquisite packaging materials from later dynasties feature among the displays. Ⓢ *Jeifang Bei Lu*
• *9am–5pm daily*
• *Adm*

Yuexiu Park

The lovely expanse of park contains a sculpture of the Five Rams, the symbol of Guangzhou, and a monument to Sun Yat-sen, the revered "father of modern China". The Municipal Museum is housed in the Zhen Hai Tower, the last remnant of the city's 14th-century walls. Ⓢ *Metro Yuexiu Gongyuan Park* • *7am–7pm* • *Adm*
• *Museum 10:15am–4pm daily* • *Adm*

White Cloud Mountain

Overlooking the city haze is a huge wooded area dominated by a series of ridges and peaks, offering open space, fresh air and cooling breezes.

Guangdong Museum of Art

Probably still China's largest art museum, with ancient and contemporary Chinese art. Ⓢ *Luhu Lu 13, Ersha Island*
• *www.gdmoa.org* • *9am–5pm Tue–Sun* • *Adm*

River Trips

Escape the fumes and look back on the city from the river. A number of operators offer cruises. Try an evening trip on the *White Swan*, a lovely old masted yacht.

Five Rams sculpture, Yeuxiu Park

Price Categories

For a three-course meal for one with half a bottle of wine (or equivalent meal) and extra charges.

$	under HK$100
$$	HK$100–$250
$$$	HK$250–$450
$$$$	HK$450–$600
$$$$$	over HK$600

1920 Restaurant and Bar

TOP 10 Places to Eat and Drink

J M Chef (aka Chao Mei)
Those of a nervous disposition may want to skip the "frog milk" and "stewed insect in pot", but the sizzling "chicken with three cups wine" is terrific.
⬥ Opp White Swan Hotel, Shamian Island • 8121 7018 • No credit cards • $$

Paddy Fields
One of the most popular expatriate hangouts, this cheekily named restaurant offers authentic, traditional Irish fare. After a diet of noodles, rack of lamb with mint sauce can come as a shock.
⬥ Central Plaza, Huale Lu 38 • 8360 1379 • $$

J M Chef

Bai Yuan Xian
A great opportunity to try – among other Cantonese and Chaozhou specialities – sweet and sour pork (tang cu li ji) as it should be. ⬥ 67 Huanshi Donglu • 8333 3998 • No credit cards • $$

Dong Jiang Hai Xian Da Jiu Lou
Occupying a full five floors, a great place to go on a seafood adventure. ⬥ 2 Qiaoguang Lu, beside Haizhu Guangchang • 8318 4901 • $$

1920 Restaurant and Bar
Expats and locals enjoy food with a strong German influence and evening jazz sessions. ⬥ Yangjiang Zhong Lu 183 • 8333 6156 • $$

G Bar
This impressive lounge is a stellar spot for pre- or post-dinner drinks with fine city views. ⬥ Grand Hyatt Guangzhou, 12 Zhujiang West Rd • 8550 8234 • $$$

Japan Fusion
In a city famed for its football-field sized restaurants, this is one of the largest. A huge choice of Japanese-Cantonese fusion dishes. ⬥ 2/F Metro Plaza, Tian He Bei Lu 358–378 • 3880 8118 • $$

Di Matteo
Guangzhou's most reliable Italian cuisine plus a very popular Sunday brunch. ⬥ West Side First Floor, Tian He Bei Lu 175–181 • 8525 0789 • $$$

Chuan Guo Yan Yi
An excellent introduction to hot and spicy Sichuan cuisine. Hotpot comes with a yin/yang-style divider for those unaccustomed to fiery foods.
⬥ 4/F Nan Fang Securities Bldg, 140–148 Tiyu Dong Lu • 3887 9878 • $$

Tang
Tang offers a very Cantonese interpretation of elaborate imperial royal recipes. Located in the same building as its popular live music venue and nightclub. ⬥ Jian Shi Liu Ma Lu 1 • 8338 2892 • $$

STREETSMART

STREETSMART

Left **Hong Kong Airport** Centre **British brand shop** Right **Road signs in Chinese and English**

TOP10 Planning Your Trip

1 Passport and Visa Information

Citizens from the UK, US, Canada, Australia and New Zealand need only a valid passport to enter Hong Kong. UK citizens may stay up to six months and US, Canadian, Australian and New Zealand visitors for up to three months without a visa. (Ensure your passport is valid for at least a month after you plan to leave Hong Kong.) To visit mainland China (beyond the New Territories), you will need a visa. These are easy to obtain from travel agents in Hong Kong. China Travel Service can process an application in a day. Visas can also be obtained at the upstairs visa office at the checkpoint on the train line before entering China. Most visitors may stay in Macau for up to 20 days without a visa – Portuguese citizens are allowed 90 days.

2 When to Go

The milder months from October to late January are a popular time to visit, although Hong Kong's climate is at its best in March and April. Hotel rooms will be heavily booked and more expensive in October and April. Flights also tend to be heavily booked during these months.

3 Climate

Just south of the Tropic of Cancer, Hong Kong's sub-tropical climate has a mild winter (December–February) when temperatures can drop as low as 10°C (50°F), while spring (March–April) and autumn (October–November) are short, warm and pleasant. In summer (May–September), temperatures average about 28°C (83°F), relative summer humidity regularly soars above 80 or 90 per cent and typhoons and tropical storms often visit.

4 What to Take

Light clothing will suffice for most of the year. A long-sleeved top is advisable for some of the arctic air conditioning; a light jacket for the winter months.

5 Languages

Cantonese, Mandarin and English are the official languages of Hong Kong. English is widely understood and spoken, but expect communication difficulties with taxi drivers and residents in remoter rural areas.

6 Health Preparations

No compulsory vaccinations are required for Hong Kong, but a yellow fever vaccination is necessary if you are visiting southern China from a yellow fever-infected area. Common medicines are readily available. Ensure you have valid medical insurance.

7 Currency Information

The local currency is the Hong Kong dollar (HK$), divided into 100 cents. Bills are issued in 20-, 50-, 100-, 500- and 1,000-dollar denominations. Coins come in 1-, 2-, 5- and 10-dollar and 10-, 20- and 50-cent denominations. Pegged to the US dollar, the exchange rate always hovers close to HK$7.8 to the US$1. HK$ are accepted in Macau but change is given in MOP$. ¥RMB are needed for mainland China.

8 Money

Take lots! Hong Kong can be expensive. There is no limit on the amount that can be changed (see also p142).

9 Local Prices

Hong Kong is not the shopper's paradise it once was. Many branded and designer goods are on a par with or even pricier than in the West. Bargains can be found, however, in the markets (see pp38–9) and warehouse outlets (see pp76 & 106).

10 Driving Licences

A valid international driving licence is required for driving and car hire.

Directory

China Travel Service
78–83 Connaught Rd,
Central • 2998 7888

Previous pages **Gardeners in central Hong Kong**

Left **Airport train** Centre **Macau Airport** Right **Passenger ferry**

🔟 Getting to Hong Kong

Direct Flights
Being a major hub, Hong Kong is well served by direct connections to much of the globe. Major cities linked by direct flights to Hong Kong include: Auckland, Sydney, Melbourne, LA, London, San Francisco, Toronto and Vancouver.

Stopovers
There are plenty of stopover options for breaking your journey. Singapore, Kuala Lumpur and Bangkok can make interesting and cheap stopover breaks if flying in from the west, or Seoul and Taipei if flying in from the east. Some carriers do not charge for arranging inbound or outbound stopovers and may offer special deals.

Booking Flights and Hotels Online
Flight and hotel deals are worth checking on the websites listed in the directory. However, Chinese domestic flights should always be bought in Hong Kong or mainland China, at prices up to 50 per cent cheaper than online. Chinese-run hotel rates are best bargained for locally.

Finding the Cheapest Flights
The cheapest times to head to Hong Kong are just after Chinese New Year and from November to mid-December. Late deals can sometimes be found on websites such as lastminute.co.uk. Booking well in advance can also secure lower prices. Some websites, such as travelocity.com, offer e-mail services alerting you when tickets fall below a certain price. Bargains are less likely if your return leg falls in August, or between Christmas and Chinese New Year.

Flights from Southeast Asia
If you'll be spending time in Southeast Asia first, very competitively priced air tickets to Hong Kong can be bought in Bangkok, Kuala Lumpur and Singapore.

Information at the Airport
There are tourist information offices in the arrivals buffer halls A and B. There's also a hotel information and reservations office in the arrivals halls.

Cross-Country Route by Rail
For those with time and money, the most adventurous way to reach Hong Kong from Europe is by rail via the Trans-Siberia Railway, through Mongolia or Manchuria to Beijing, and then connecting to Hong Kong.

Rail Routes from China
Hong Kong-bound trains depart several times daily from Guangzhou East. Sleeper services from Beijing and Shanghai depart on alternate days. "Soft" sleeper compartments are plush and less crowded but beware, they can cost almost as much as flying.

By Sea
Fast, regular ferry services to Hong Kong run from Guangzhou and Macau. Services from Macau take between one and two hours and from Guangzhou two to three hours.

By Road
Several buses also run daily between Guangzhou and Hong Kong.

Directory

Websites
www.agoda.com
www.expedia.com
www.priceline.com
www.priceline.co.uk
www.travelocity.com
www.cheaptickets.com
www.bargainflights.com
www.lastminute.co.uk
www.cathaypacific.com

Airport Information
General information booths 2181 8888 or 2508 1234
• 8am–6pm daily
• www.hkairport.com
• Hotel reservation desks 6am–1am daily

Left **MTR logo** Centre **Taxi** Right **Tram**

🔟 Getting Around Hong Kong

1 Airport Transfer Options

The excellent, modern airport trains to Central take just 24 minutes and depart every 12 minutes from 5:50am to 1:15am daily. Taxis are also readily available at the airport. The E11 bus through Central, Wanchai and Causeway Bay takes about an hour and is the cheapest option.

2 Octopus Cards

If you're going to travel widely in Hong Kong consider buying an Octopus card, which you charge with money and swipe over the readers on most local buses, trains, ferries and trams. Special tourist versions allow unlimited travel for 24 hours or three days.

3 The MTR

The excellent, efficient MTR (Mass Transit Railway) system runs from about 5:30am until 1am. There are currently 11 lines, linking Hong Kong Island and Kowloon with Lantau, the airport and the New Territories right up to the Chinese border. All lines are clean, cheap and easy to use; all except the Light Rail are air-conditioned. MRT ticket machines have English instructions.

4 Buses

Cheap, frequent buses connect almost every place in Hong Kong. Pick up a bus route map at any of the HKTA's offices. Major hotels offer free shuttle buses between the hotels and Kowloon and Central Airport Express stations.

5 Taxis

Red taxis operate in and around central Hong Kong and are reasonably priced. Surcharges apply for tunnel tolls, luggage in the trunk and late-night journeys. Tipping is not expected. Green taxis run in the New Territories; blue ones on Lantau. Bear in mind though that few taxi drivers can speak much English.

6 Ferries

Ferries link Hong Kong Island with Kowloon, the outlying islands, Macau and China. The frequent Star Ferries (see pp14–15) shuttle between Hong Kong and Tsim Sha Tsui on Kowloon from 6:30am to 11:30pm. Next to Central's Star Ferry pier are the main piers for outlying islands.

7 Trams

The ancient, wood-panelled, double-deck trams running west to east from Kennedy Town to Chai Wan are a slow, sometimes cramped but undeniably atmospheric way to get around Hong Kong. A very reasonable flat fee applies for all destinations. The legendary Peak Tram (see p9) leaves from Garden Road.

8 On Foot

The best way to see many central Hong Kong districts is to walk. The distances are short, although the inclines can be steep. Walking is really the only way to see the sights in Western, the Mid-Levels, Wan Chai, much of Kowloon and Hong Kong's country parks. Walking in parts of Central and Admiralty, can, however, be a disorientating trudge around a maze of walkways and underpasses.

9 By Bike

Forget cycling among the urban congestion and fumes, but think about hiring a bike to hit some of the rugged, steep country trails. Contact the Hong Kong Cycling Association for details.

🔟 Car Hire and Driving

Why hire a car in Hong Kong when it's so easy to get around, parking is scarce and congestion is so intense? If you do, you'll need an international driving licence.

Directory

Hong Kong Cycling Association
2504 8176

Car Hire
Avis 2620 0586, www.avis.com • Hertz 2525 1313, www.hertz.com • Trinity 2563 6117

Left **Octopus travel cards** Centre **Tourist information sign** Right **HKTB desk**

🔟 Sources of Information

1 HKTB Services

The Hong Kong Tourism Board (HKTB) has conveniently located branches offering brochures and advice. There is also a website and multilingual visitor hotline.

2 Websites

HKTB's website *(see directory)* is a good starting point. Others include the *South China Morning Post's* www.scmp.com and traveldk.com/hong-kong. For directory services go to www.hkt.com.

3 Newspapers

The broadsheet daily *South China Morning Post* provides extensive coverage of local, Chinese and world news. The tabloid *Standard* gives less comprehensive coverage and an irreverent spin.

4 Local Magazines

The best local listings magazine is the bi-monthly *Time Out Hong Kong*. There's also the free weekly *HK Magazine* with eating, drinking and going out tips and *BC Magazine* (also free) for club-goers.

5 English-Language Radio and TV

ATV World and TVB Pearl are Hong Kong's two terrestrial English-language channels. RTHK is Hong Kong's publicly funded but editorially independent radio broadcaster. RTHK 3 (567 AM, 1584AM) has

mainly news, finance and current affairs; RTHK 4 (96.7–98.9FM) plays Western and Chinese classical music, RTHK 6 (675AM) broadcasts BBC World Service programming.

6 Practical Books and Maps

The HKTB has free maps of central Hong Kong and free booklets including *A Guide to Quality Merchants, Hong Kong Access Guide for Disabled Visitors* and *Exploring Hong Kong's Countryside*, available in several languages. Good maps (the *Countryside Series*) are available from Government Publications Centres.

7 Business Information

The Hong Kong Trade Development Council (www.hktdc.com) offers useful information.

8 Facts and Figures

The government website, www.gov.hk, with links to all its departments, is a good starting point for facts and figures. The CIA's online World Factbook offers raw statistics on Hong Kong and China at: www.cia.gov/cia/publications/factbook/index.html

9 Weather and Air Quality Info

Hong Kong Observatory's phoneline and website offer daily and three-day forecasts. The Weather Underground site,

www.underground.org.hk, and *South China Morning Post* at http://weather.scmp.com also have local weather and air pollution information.

10 Some Books for Background

Hong Kong: A Guide to Recent Architecture by Juanita Cheng and Andrew Yeoh is a useful pocket guide. *A History of Hong Kong* by Frank Welsh starts from the time of British rule. *Travellers' Tales Guides: Hong Kong* includes some excellent writing from Jan Morris, Bruce Chatwin and Charles Jennings.

Directory

HKTB Website
www.hktb.com

HKTB Branches
Airport buffer halls and Area E2
• *Tsim Sha Tsui Star Ferry terminal, Kowloon, 8am–6pm daily*
• *Causeway Bay MTR station, 8am–8pm daily*

HKTB Hotline
2508 1234

Government Publications Centres
4/F Murray Building, Garden Rd, Central, 2537 1910

HK Observatory
2926 8200
• *www.weather.gov.hk*

Left **Busy road in Central** Right **Topless bar signs** Right **Public bus**

🔟 Things to Avoid

1 Driving in Central Hong Kong and Kowloon
Traffic is often bumper to bumper, so walk or take another form of transport.

2 Hurrying in Central on a Sunday
Filipino and Indonesian domestic workers crowd Central's sidewalks and squares on a Sunday, so don't expect anything other than slow progress. Watching these low-paid workers enjoying their only day off makes for a contrast, or perhaps rebuke, to the bustle and conspicuous consumption usually on display.

3 The Peak on a Sunday
Long queues form for the Peak Tram and the whole Peak area is much busier at weekends and particularly on Sundays. Turn round and come back another day if it's cloudy, too, as you'll miss those spectacular views.

4 Eating or Drinking on the MTR
Hong Kongers may blithely litter their streets, countryside and harbour, but no-one eats or drinks on the spotless subway.

5 Hostess Bars of Wanchai or Tsim Sha Tsui
That is unless you want to pay steep surprise cover charges on top of your already expensive drinks. These may still be popular destinations for US sailors on shore leave, but don't expect to recapture the world of Suzy Wong.

6 Illegal Drug Use
Expect to be arrested if you are found in possession of illegal drugs of any kind. Hong Kong law officially makes no distinction between the types of drug found. Spot checks and raids are sometimes carried out in areas such as Lan Kwai Fong.

7 Unfamiliar Areas Late at Night
There's no doubt Hong Kong is a relatively safe city, but don't tempt fate by wandering through quiet streets and heavily built-up housing areas in the dead of night. Take a taxi instead.

8 Traffic-Choked Areas
On smoggy days you can see, smell and taste the pollution in places such as Causeway Bay and Central. When the pollution index heads above 100, escape the smog by taking a trip out to the countryside or the outlying islands.

9 Taking a Bus Without the Right Change
No change is offered on buses, so take the right money, use an Octopus Card (see p138) or be prepared to lose the change owed to you.

10 Leaving a Rucksack Unattended
Backpackers staying in places like the Chungking Mansions (see p152) should take particular care with rucksacks. Theft by unscrupulous fellow travellers is a possibility.

Directory

General Emergencies
999

Crime Hotline
2527 7177

Hospital Authority Enquiry Service
2300 6555
• www.ha.org.hk

The Adventist Hospital
40 Stubs Rd, Happy Valley, Hong Kong Island • 3651 8888

Caritas Medical Centre
111 Wing Hong St, Sham Shui Po
• 3408 5678

Matilda Hospital
41 Mount Kellet Rd, The Peak, Hong Kong Island • 2849 0111

Queen Mary Hospital
102 Pok Fu Lam Rd, Hong Kong Island
• 2255 3111

Lost/Stolen Credit Cards
Amex 2811 6122
• MasterCard 800 966 677 toll free • VISA 800 900 782

Left **Crowded street scene** Centre **Hiking, the Wilson trail** Right **Traditional pharmacy**

🔟 Health and Security Tips

1 Foreign-Language Hotlines

Important information and emergency hotlines are efficient and provide foreign-language speakers – mainly English.

2 Drinking Water and Food Safety

Hong Kong's tap water is safe to drink. Wash fresh fruit and vegetables. Avoid locally caught seafood if your health is fragile, as high pollution levels and some diseases can lurk in local fish. Many local restaurants source fish from abroad.

3 Air Pollution Advice

Urban air quality is improving rapidly following the introduction of cleaner vehicle fuels. Even so, the air pollution index can still head above 100, at which point people with respiratory complaints are advised to stay indoors. Consult the SCMP's website http://weather.scmp.com for regular updates.

4 Seawater Pollution and Swimming Dangers

Sadly, Hong Kong has made slow progress in treating the sewage it empties into its own waters, let alone in tackling the pollution washing from China's rivers. There are good beaches (usually government managed) but seawater quality can vary markedly. Toxic algae blooms occasionally make swimming unsafe. It's best to swim on a lifeguard-staffed beach with shark net. On unmanaged beaches never swim at dawn, dusk, in murky waters or with open wounds.

5 Avoiding Security Risks

Crime and theft directed at tourists are rare in Hong Kong. To be completely safe, take common-sense precautions like keeping a close hold on personal possessions, using a hotel safe if provided and not leaving valuable items or documents in your backpack.

6 Other Security Precautions

If you are planning to spend time in Hong Kong, registering your passport with your local consulate or embassy will make replacing a lost one easier. Extra travel insurance may be a good idea if you are travelling with expensive items.

7 Heat and Humidity Precautions

Hydration is important at all times, especially so in Hong Kong's stifling summer heat and humidity. Ensure you drink plenty of fluid. Cool, light, loose cotton clothing will be most comfortable. Wear a hat if you are outdoors for long periods or turn your umbrella into a sun parasol. If you're worried about the heat, avoid too much activity during the hottest part of the day. Head up Victoria Peak for cooler climes or to the coast for sea breezes.

8 What to Take if Hiking

Don't underestimate your ability to sweat and lose fluid in the heat. Take lots of water. Buy a good map, take a mobile phone if you have one and small change for local transport. Sensible clothing and footwear are a must for walking unpaved trails. Pocket tissues might come in handy for some of the public toilets in rustic areas. In winter, take a waterproof.

9 Hospitals with A&E

Caritas Medical Centre and Queen Mary Hospital are among those with 24-hour accident and emergency departments.

10 Doctors and Dentists

The Adventist Hospital and the Matilda Hospital are both private hospitals with bilingual (Cantonese/English) staff. Their outpatient departments include those for women and travellers, and there are also maternity and dental clinics. See the *Yellow Pages* for more foreign-language doctors and dentists in Hong Kong.

Left **Bank window** Centre left **ATM** Centre right **Phone boxes** Right **Man on a mobile**

Banking and Communications

Banks, ATMs and Credit Cards
Banks and ATMs are numerous. Opening hours are 9am–4:30pm Mon–Fri and 9am–12:30pm Sat. Most ATMs operate 24 hours. Credit/debit cards are widely accepted.

Money Changing and Forwarding
Using your bank card at an ATM may be cheaper than changing money or using travellers' cheques. Money forwarding can be arranged through local banks or Western Union.

Post
The Hong Kong postal service is rapid and efficient. Local mail takes one to two days. Zone 1 air mail (all of Asia except Japan) takes three to five days. Zone 2 (the rest of the world) takes five to seven days. The General Post Office operates Hong Kong's post restante service.

Telephones
Local calls in Hong Kong are free. Many hotel lobbies and shops will make phones available free for local calls. Coin-operated public phone boxes cost HK$1 minimum. Some accept credit cards or have Internet services. Phone cards for calling abroad are available from conve-nience stores, some vending machines, the Star Ferry piers and HKTB offices (see p139).

Calling Hong Kong
The international code for Hong Kong is 852, for Macau 853, and for mainland China 86. Hong Kong and Macau have no area or city codes, but Guangzhou is 020 and Shenzhen 0755.

Mobile Phones
Hong Kong's mobile networks are GSM-based, and cellular phones from almost anywhere will work. However, North Americans will need an unlocked tri- or quad-band phone. Several local companies sell pay-as-you-go SIM cards, which are much cheaper to use than the tariffs charged by your service supplier.

Local Internet Access
Internet access is plentiful, convenient, cheap and often free (see p143). Much of Hong Kong uses speedy broadband connections, including the main hotels. Some cafés and bars, public parks and cultural centres offer free Wi-Fi.

Hong Kong Central Library
Hundreds of magazines and newspapers from around the world are available to read free at the main library in Causeway Bay. Internet access here is plentiful, fast and free (bookings are taken for one hour slots at a time). There's

also a good café here with outdoor seating.

Faxing
Faxing from business centres or photocopying shops is simple, although not cheap. Your hotel may offer a cheaper service and will accept faxes on your behalf.

Business Facilities
Hong Kong is well supplied with business centres and services. See Hong Kong's Yellow Pages. Business cards can be printed on Man Wa Lane in Sheung Wan, off Des Voeux Road West. Have your details translated into Chinese on the back.

Directory

Collect Calls
10010

Directory Services
1081

General Post Office
2 Connaught Place,
HK Island • 2921 2222

PCCW Phone Rental
2888 0008

Main Library
66 Causeway Bay Rd,
HK Island • 2921 0208

Western Union
Star Ferry 2117 9088
• www.westernunion.
com.hk

United Centre
95 Queensway,
HK Island

Left **Temple** Centre **Cheap food stall** Right **Tai Chi**

TOP 10 Hong Kong on a Budget

1 Eating Cheap
Food kiosks and inexpensive Chinese restaurants abound. Fast food chains are competitive in Hong Kong. Lunchtime all-you-can-eat buffets are also fairly common, or head to the Reclamation Street Canteens at Temple Street Night Market for cheap noodles and rice dishes *(see p19)*.

2 Cheap Nights Out
Most bars offer long happy hours or promotions before a certain time of evening. Drink is free for women on certain nights at numerous bars. On race nights, soak up the atmosphere and some cheap beer at Happy Valley horseracing track *(see pp12–13)*.

3 Cheap Days Out
There are plenty of options for cheap days out. Walk Hong Kong's wilderness trails *(see pp46–7)*, nose around the market at Stanley *(see p16)*, or walk the Dragon's Back path to Shek O *(see p74)*. It need only cost the return bus fare and the price of a cheap lunch, which you can sleep off on the beach.

4 Free Buildings, Museums and Galleries
For dizzying views atop some of the world's tallest buildings head to the free viewing gallery on the 43rd floor of the Bank of China Building in Central *(see p42)*. Hong Kong's museums and galleries are incredibly cheap to visit, but all have a free day each week and some are free all week.

5 Free Parks and Gardens
Hong Kong Park *(see p59)*, which includes the excellent walk-through Edward Youde Aviary, and the Zoological and Botanical Gardens *(see p54)* nearby are well worth a visit and are completely free.

6 Free Tai Chi Lessons
Learn the slow, graceful, health-promoting moves of the traditional Chinese martial art Tai Chi for free in front of the Museum of Art early on Monday, Wednesday, Thursday and Friday mornings *(see also p33)*.

7 Temples
Hong Kong's many temples are free (although change for the collection box is appreciated). Try the Man Mo Temple on Hollywood Road *(see p61)*, the Tin Hau Temple off Nathan Road in Yau Ma Tei *(see p89)* or the Wong Tai Sin Temple in eastern Kowloon *(see p95)*.

8 Free Calls and Internet Access
Local telephone calls are usually free, except from payphones and many hotel rooms. Some hotel lobbies have telephones for free local calls. Internet access is plentiful and free at the Convention Centre's Business Centre, at the Causeway Bay Main Library and at some cafés and bars.

9 Free Cultural Events
For free music go to the foyer of the Hong Kong Cultural Centre *(see p82)* on Thursday lunchtimes and some Saturdays. The Fringe Club *(see p64)* hosts free live music from local and visiting bands on certain weekends. Free exhibitions of local artists' and photographers' work are always on at the Hong Kong Arts Centre in Tsim Sha Tsui.

10 Bargain Basement Accommodation
For central and cheap, if sometimes nasty, accommodation, try the labyrinthine Chungking Mansions *(see p82)* or its grubby little sister Mirador Mansions, both on Nathan Road in Tsim Sha Tsui. Also consider the YMCA and Youth Hostel Association *(see also pp146, 151 & 152)*.

Directory

YMCA
2268 7000

Youth Hostel Association
2788 3105

Left **Cobbler** Centre **Landmark Centre** Right **Souvenir opera mask**

TOP 10 Shopping Tips

Opening Hours
Most shops open daily but not usually before 10:30am and will not generally close before 6:30pm. Many, especially in the busy shopping districts, close later at 9pm or beyond.

Sales Tax
After attempts to introduce a broad GST levy were ditched in 2006, Hong Kong has no sales taxes except on cars, cosmetics, alcohol and tobacco.

When to Haggle
Small businesses, such as the many independent computer and electrical goods stores, are often worth trying to bargain with. Consider asking for a cash discount for items such as computers or antiques. Haggling is almost obligatory in the markets, particularly for antiques and souvenirs.

QTS Symbol
Where you see the QTS symbol (a large gold Q with black brushstroke), it indicates the shop has passed a Hong Kong Productivity Council Audit for fair trading, service levels, store environment and product knowledge.

Finding Larger Sizes
Some Westerners, women in particular, find shoes designed for the slighter Asian foot a tight fit. It's worth asking boutiques and shops if they have your size in their warehouse. Clothes are usually less of a problem. Hong Kong's Marks & Spencer outlets provide a wide range of clothing sizes.

Finding a Tailor
Dozens of tailors can hand-make suits in as little as 48 hours. The prices can be good, although a cheap deal sometimes means cheap cloth or corners cut. If in doubt use a better-known tailor. For men's suits try the famous Sam's Tailor or the Mandarin Hotel's bespoke A-Man Hing Cheong. For tailor-made *cheong sams*, try funky Shanghai Tang.

Shopping on a Budget
For dirt-cheap clothes, head to the markets at Lai Chi Kok and Sham Shui Po. The ubiquitous Giordano and Bossini chains offer good-value Gap-style wear. For deeply discounted clearance designer wear head to the shops on the 4th, 5th and 6th floors of the Pedder Building on Pedder St in Central or Joyce's warehouse outlet on Ap Lei Chau *(see p76)*.

Break for the Border
Consider getting a visa for China *(see p136)* and cross over to the border town of Shenzhen *(see pp126–9)* for cheap clothes and designer fakes. If you're prepared to haggle for each and every purchase and do a lot of shopping, the trip will pay for itself.

Fakes
Fake designer clothes and watches are cheap, common and easy to find in any of Hong Kong's markets and especially in Shenzhen. Quality can range from the good to the dreadful, so buyer beware.

Avoiding Rip-Offs
Take great care when buying complicated items such as cameras, computers and other electronics, particularly from the independent shops in Tsim Sha Tsui. Is there a warranty? If yes, can the item be serviced or repaired under it once you are back home? Are essential accessories included?

Directory

A-Man Hing Cheong
*Mandarin Oriental,
5 Connaught Rd,
Central, Hong Kong
Island* • 2522 3336

Sam's Tailor
*94 Nathan Rd, Tsim
Sha Tsui* • 2367 9423

Shanghai Tang
*1 Duddell St, Central,
Hong Kong Island*
• 2525 7333

Left **Happy Valley** Right **Tsing Ma suspension bridge**

TOP 10 Tours

1 Bus-Based Tours
If time is short or legs tire, the 5-hour Heritage Tour offers a whistlestop glimpse of ancient temples, ancestral clan halls and walled villages. The daily Land Between Tour takes in Hong Kong's highest mountain, and various rural markets and fishing villages. HKTB can provide booking numbers.

2 Cultural Kaleidoscope
This innovative and free series of walks and lectures by a group of experts on local culture, traditional Chinese medicine and feng shui, offers some excellent insights into traditional Hong Kong and Chinese culture. A daily talk is held at a set location covering a different topic each day. Get details from the HKTB.

3 DIY Walking Tours
It may be a stone's throw from Central's skyscrapers, but the self-guided Western Walking Tour takes you into a different world past dried seafood shops, herbalists and temples. Pick up a brochure from HKTB offices. A more remote alternative is the Lung Yuek Tau Heritage Trail, a short but fascinating walk starting at Fung Ying Sin Koon Temple, which passes elegant ancestral halls, and tiny, still-inhabited walled villages.

4 Hong Kong Dolphinwatch
You're almost guaranteed to see Hong Kong's endangered pink dolphins off Lantau Island on this four-hour tour, and if you don't you can go again free. Learn from the knowledgeable guides about the lives of these creatures and the threats they face.

5 Museums and Galleries
See all of Hong Kong's museums and galleries the easy way via the bus that shuttles between the art, science, space and history museums in Tsim Sha Tsui and the smart, impressive Heritage Museum at Sha Tin. A one-week bus pass with unlimited entry ticket to all museums is available from HKTB offices. The special bus runs on Wednesday, Friday and Sunday from 10am to 6pm.

6 Harbour Tours
Take in the skyline of Central from the harbour by day or night, or sail beneath the Tsing Ma suspension bridge. A range of harbour cruises is on offer. Visit HKTB offices for details.

7 Horseracing Tour
Feel the earth move and the hooves thunder as you cheer the finishers home in the ultimate Hong Kong night out. Splendid Tours runs the Come Horseracing Tour during race meetings *(see pp12–13 & 101).*

8 Local Rambles
Details of local walks can be found on HKTB's website: www.hktb.com, and in a brochure published twice a year and available for free from HKTB offices in Hong Kong and overseas.

9 Junk Hire
If money is no object, hire a junk for the day and explore Hong Kong's secluded beaches and craggy islands. See the *Yellow Pages* for listings.

10 Helicopter Rides
For the most dramatic perspectives of Hong Kong, HKTB recommends Grayline Tours' 15-minute helicopter ride, followed by lunch, a sampan ride and a tram ride to the Peak. Heliservices AirTours also offer 30-minute and 1-hour rides over the harbour, Kowloon and Lantau.

Directory

HKTB
Visitor hotline 7am–9pm daily • 2508 1234

Hong Kong Dolphinwatch
2984 1414

Grayline Tours
2368 7111

Heliservices AirTours
2802 0200

Left **YMCA** Centre **Waiter, Peninsula Hotel** Right **Pool, The Peninsula**

🔟 Accommodation Tips

1 Making Reservations

Booking through the HKTB or a travel agent will almost always be cheaper than just turning up at a hotel. Many websites offer hotel reservation services (see also p137). The Hong Kong Hotel Association runs reservations lines.

2 High Season

Rates climb during the busy conference months of October and April, and the best hotels (and many of the rest) will be booked solid. Avoid these months if you can, or book long in advance.

3 What's Included in the Price

Use of facilities such as gyms and pools are usually included in the room price. Breakfast is seldom included in the price except at top-of-the-range places. Note that a 3 per cent government tax and a 10 per cent service charge will be added to your bill at all but the lowest-priced guesthouses. Local calls are free from public phones in Hong Kong, but strangely not usually from your hotel room.

4 Good Cheap Accommodation

Don't be put off by the name, the YMCA (see p151) in Tsim Sha Tsui is well appointed and offers terrific views and value.

Or try the two-star Anne Black Guest House close to the Temple Street area in Kowloon. (See also other entries pp151–2.)

5 Late Arrivals

If you've just got off the plane and need a place, try the hotel information and reservations offices in arrivals halls A and B, open from 6am to 1pm or make for Chungking or Mirador Mansions on Nathan Road (see p152).

6 Useful Websites

The websites listed in the directory are easy to use and book through, with plenty of substantial deals and discounts of up to 65 per cent.

7 Single Travellers

The Anne Black Guest House has plenty of clean, cheap single rooms. Less appealing (but half the price) guesthouses such as in the Chungking Mansions (see p152) are other good budget options for single travellers.

8 Families

Most of the better hotels offer babysitting services. The YMCA (see p151) has a few competitively priced family suites.

9 Long-Stay Deals

Many hotels and guesthouses will offer excellent discounts for stays of a month or more. For long stays it may be worth renting a serviced apartment (below). The Wesley in Wan Chai offers very competitive monthly packages. (See also p153.)

10 Apartotels

The Shama Group offers Central serviced apartments. If you want to get away from it all, some small, basic holiday apartments can be rented on leafy, low-rise Lamma Island close to the beaches, bars and restaurants.

Directory

HK Hotel Association
Info 2375 3838
• Reservations 2769 8822 or 2383 8380
• www.hkha.org

Anne Black Guest House
2713 9211

Websites
• www.accomline.com
• www.agoda.com
• www.asiatravel.com
• www.lastminute.com
• www.rentaroomhk.com

Shama Group
3100 8555
• www.shama.com

YMCA
41 Salisbury Rd, Tsim Sha Tsui
• 2268 7000

The Wesley
22 Hennessy Rd, Wan Chai • 2866 6688

Price Categories

For a standard, double room per night (with breakfast if included), taxes and extra charges.

$	under HK$500
$$	HK$500–$1,000
$$$	HK$1,000–$2,000
$$$$	HK$2,000–$2,500
$$$$$	over HK$2,500

Left **Bar, Island Shangri-La** Right **The Mandarin Oriental HK**

Super Luxury Hotels

The Peninsula
Opened in 1928 and still one of Hong Kong's best-loved hotels, the Neo-Classical Peninsula overlooking Victoria Harbour is famous for restrained luxury and excellent, friendly service (see p81). ✆ Salisbury Rd, Kowloon • Map N4 • 2920 2888 • www.peninsula.com • $$$$$

The Mandarin Oriental HK
In an excellent location in the heart of the financial district, this fashionable hotel overlooks Victoria Harbour. The bustling public areas are one of the territory's most popular meeting places, while the rooms have an elegant atmosphere and a modern, luxurious design, which incorporates every conceivable high-tech convenience. ✆ 5 Connaught Rd, Central • Map K4 • 2522 0111 • www.mandarinoriental.com • $$$$$

Hotel Inter-Continental Hong Kong
Popular with the rich and famous, the splendid, modern InterContinental (formerly the Regent) is consistently voted among Asia's best hotels. The huge, beautifully appointed rooms offer fantastic harbour views. ✆ 18 Salisbury Rd, Kowloon • Map N4 • 2721 1211 • www.ichotelsgroup.com • $$$$$

Island Shangri-La
The grandiose lobby, huge chandeliers and stunning silk landscape adorning the atrium are a prelude to the elegantly decorated rooms, with terrific Peak or harbour views. ✆ Pacific Place, Central • Map M6 • 2877 3838 • www.shangri-la.com • $$$$$

The Conrad
Guests are dwarfed by the giant flowers and insects on the high lobby murals in this impressive hotel. Rooms above the 40th floor are large and sumptuous, with excellent harbour or Peak views. ✆ Pacific Place, Central • Map M6 • 2521 3838 • www.conrad.com.hk • $$$$$

The Grand Hyatt
Next to the Convention Centre and the premier choice for unbridled luxury in Wan Chai, the Grand Hyatt has looked after world-famous guests including former US President Clinton. Rooms have a modern feel, including all high-tech mod-cons. ✆ 1 Harbour Rd, Wan Chai • Map N5 • 2588 1234 • www.hongkong.grand.hyatt.com • $$$$$

The Landmark Mandarin Oriental
A stylish conversion of former offices has created some of the largest rooms in Asia, all with circular sunken baths, HD TVs and broadband. ✆ 15 Queen's Rd Central, Central • Map L5 • 2132 0188 • www.mandarinoriental.com • $$$$$

The Venetian
Macau's most spectacular hotel-casino is a repeat of the Las Vegas dream of Italy, but with sampans among the gondolas. The mega-resort is suites only, and has a themed shopping mall and a 1,800-seat theatre. ✆ Estrada da Baía de N Senhora da Esperança, Cotai Strip, Macau • 2882 8888 • www.venetianmacau.com • $$$$$

Kowloon Shangri-La
Not quite up to the standards of its Hong Kong Island counterpart, perhaps, but the Kowloon Shangri-La offers luxury at a significant discount to its sister. The Horizon Club tariff includes butler service and club lounge. ✆ 64 Mody Rd, Kowloon • Map P3 • 2721 2111 • www.shangri-la.com • $$$$$

The Langham
Restrained opulence reigns throughout. There's a good gym, pool and sauna, and top-quality restaurants, including the impressive Cantonese T'ang Court, decked out like a Mongolian tent. ✆ 8 Peking Road, Tsim Sha Tsui, Kowloon • Map M4 • 2375 1133 • www.langhamhotels.com • $$$$

Note: Unless otherwise stated, all hotels accept credit cards, have en-suite bathrooms and air conditioning

Left **Ritz-Carlton Hong Kong** Centre **Banyan Tree Macau** Right **Hullett House**

🔟 Luxury Hotels

Wynn Macau
This vast casino resort features high-ceilinged, tastefully decorated rooms with sweeping views. The interior feel is more that of a stylish friend's apartment than a hotel room, with hidden flat-screen TVs and electronic controls for everything. ✆ *Rua Cidade de Sintra, NAPE, Macau • 2888 9966 • www.wynnmacau.com • $$$$*

Hullett House
The blend of superb heritage architecture and contemporary interiors make this Hong Kong's top boutique hotel. Located in the former headquarters of the Marine Police, there are 10 exquisitely designed rooms with superb facilities as well as a fabulous stone terrace overlooking the Heritage 1881 courtyard. ✆ *2A Canton Rd, Tsim Sha Tsui • Map M4 • 3988 0000 • www.hulletthouse.com • $$$$$*

Ritz-Carlton, Guangzhou
The city's finest luxury hotel is located in Pearl River City opposite the soaring Guangzhou Tower. Superlative luxury, superb amenities and classic Ritz-Carlton service help to explain why its room rates are also top dollar. ✆ *3 Xing An Rd, Guangzhou • Map L2 • 3813 6688 • www.ritzcarlton.com • $$$$*

Banyan Tree Macau
With great views of Macau's skyline, this magnificent resort hotel is supremely luxurious in style and amenities. Both the restaurants and the spa are of the highest quality. ✆ *Galaxy Macau Resort, Avenida Marginal Flor de Lotus, Cotai Strip • 2721 5215 • www.banyantree.com/en/macau • $$$$$*

Garden Hotel Guangzhou
The cavernous lobby gives some sense of the size of this imposing 1,000-plus room hotel, boasting its own up-market shopping mall and good eating and drinking options. ✆ *368 Huangshi Dong Lu, Guangzhou • 8333 8989 • www.thegardenhotel.com.cn • $$$*

The Upper House
This hotel has beautifully styled rooms with superb views and great facilities. Café Gray restaurant and lounge on the 49th floor is a regular watering hole for Hong Kong's fashionable set. ✆ *Pacific Place, 88 Queensway, Central • Map M4 • 3968 1111 • www.upperhouse.com • $$$$$*

The Excelsior
The smart, modern and friendly Excelsior offers pretty much every in-room and hotel facility imaginable, as you'd expect from the Mandarin Oriental's sister. ✆ *281 Gloucester Rd, Causeway Bay • Map Q5 • 2894 8888 • www.excelsiorhongkong.com • $$$$*

The Sheraton
Rooms are comfortable but hardly special. However, the hotel's central waterfront position, and full range of facilities including gym, pool, spa and 24-hour movie channels, put it in the luxury category. ✆ *20 Nathan Rd, Kowloon • Map N4 • 2369 1111 • www.sheraton.com • $$$$$*

Shangri-La Hotel Shenzhen
Close to the main shopping areas and railway station, the Shangri-la makes a great escape from Shenzhen's seething retail madness. The rooftop pool (with gym, sauna and steam room nearby) makes a good place to relax. ✆ *Jianshe Lu, Shenzhen • Map D1 • 8233 0888 • www.shangri-la.com • $$*

Ritz-Carlton, Hong Kong
The views are incredible throughout this hotel in Hong Kong's tallest building. The quality of design and in-room technology place it at the summit of modern luxury hotels. ✆ *International Commerce Centre, 1 Austin Rd West, Kowloon • Map L2 • 2263 2263 • www.ritzcarlton.com • $$$$$*

➤ **Note:** *Unless otherwise stated, all hotels accept credit cards, have en-suite bathrooms and air conditioning*

Price Categories

For a standard,
double room per
night (with breakfast
if included), taxes
and extra charges.

$ under HK$500
$$ HK$500–$1,000
$$$ HK$1,000–$2,000
$$$$ HK$2,000–$2,500
$$$$$ over HK$2,500

Left **Kowloon Hotel** Right **Regal Airport Hotel**

🔟 Mid-Range Hotels in Hong Kong

1 The Renaissance Harbour View

The location above the Convention and Exhibition Centre on the waterfront ensures its popularity as a business hotel, but its landscaped grounds and leisure facilities are a draw for all. 🕙 *1 Harbour Rd, Wanchai • Map N5 • 2802 8888 • www. marriott.com • $$$$$*

2 Kowloon Hotel

Part of the Harbour Plaza group, the Kowloon is well suited to business travellers and people seeking a good location and connectivity. Its high-tech rooms boast computers with Internet access. Rooms are smallish though, and the supposedly digital/tech-look is starting to look unintentionally retro 80s. 🕙 *19–21 Nathan Road, Tsim Sha Tsui, Kowloon • Map N4 • 2929 2888 • www. harbour-plaza.com • $$$*

3 Empire Hotel Kowloon

Opened in late 2001, this very smart hotel with a modern gym and a lovely atrium pool is a complete contrast to its threadbare sister in Wan Chai. Rooms are equipped with the latest Internet and audio-visual gadgetry. The location is perfect for Tsim Sha Tsui shopping and dining. 🕙 *62 Kimberley Road, Tsim Sha Tsui • Map N3 • 3692 2222 • www.empirehotel. com.hk • $$$*

4 Hyatt Regency

Located in one of Kowloon's tallest hotels, this impressive hotel is aimed at both business and leisure travellers. Rooms on the upper floors boast exceptional views out over Hong Kong and the hotel provides a great location for all the attractions on offer in Kowloon. 🕙 *18 Hanoi Rd, Tsim Sha Tsui • Map N4 • 2311 1234 • hongkong.tsimshatsui@ hyatt.com • $$$*

5 Regal Airport Hotel

Hong Kong's largest hotel links directly to the airport terminal and features large rooms with avant-garde interior designs. Ten restaurants and bars provide a choice of cuisine. 🕙 *9 Cheong Tat Rd, Chek Lap Kok • Map B5 • 2286 8888 • www.regal hotel.com • $$$*

6 The Mira

Chic, slick, futuristic and maybe lacking a little soul, however you cannot help admiring the redesign of this well-maintained business hotel. The infinity-edge pool and luxury spa are definite attractions. 🕙 *118 Nathan Rd, Tsim Sha Tsui • Map N3 • 2368 1111 • www.themirahotel.com • $$$*

7 The Luxe Manor

This stylish Kowloon boutique hotel combines eclectic, almost surreal decor, with high-tech features. The rooms are decorated with painted picture frames, which climb the walls onto the ceiling. Additional features include Wi-Fi and rain showers. 🕙 *39 Kimberley Rd, Tsim Sha Tsui • Map N3 • 3763 8888 • www. theluxemanor.com • $$$*

8 The Eaton Hotel

Easily the best option in the Yau Ma Tei/Jordan area. Rooms are smart and the lobby offers a flood of natural light, outdoor seating and an oasis of greenery. 🕙 *380 Nathan Rd • Map N1 • 2782 1818 • www. eaton-hotel.com • $$$*

9 J Plus Boutique Hotel

This hotel was originally the JIA Boutique Hotel styled by the French designer Philippe Starck. The studios and one-room suites are the perfect blend of comfort and luxury. 🕙 *1–5 Irving St, Causeway Bay • Map Q6 • 3196 9000 • www. jplushongkong.com • $$$*

10 The Fleming

The perfect option for families, The Fleming has smart rooms that are reasonably priced. Many also have small kitchens. Located close to the conference centre and the ferries to Kowloon and Wan Chai. 🕙 *41 Fleming Rd, Wan Chai • Map N6 • 3607 2288 • www. thefleming.com.hk • $$$$*

Streetsmart

Left **Holiday Inn Macau** Centre **The Metropole** Right **New Century Hotel**

🔟 Mid-Range Hotels, Macau & China

1 Holiday Inn

Close by Lisboa's many casinos and convenient for the centre of Macau. Rooms (with cable) are blandly furnished but there's a good range of facilities, including gym, pool, sauna and a decent restaurant for Cantonese and Szechuan food. ✎ *82–86 Rua de Pequim, Macau • 2878 3333 • www. holidayinn.com • $$*

2 The Metropole

The sense that you've travelled back to the 1970s can be fun, but otherwise this ageing hotel, aimed more at Chinese mainlanders than foreigners, is nothing special. Happily, prices are low and it's next to some of Macau's best shopping and sightseeing areas. ✎ *Avenida de Praia Grande, Macau • 2838 8166 • www. mctshmi.com • $$*

3 Hotel Royal Macau

The Hotel Royal is one of Macau's oldest hotels and shows it. That said, it is clean and well run, although the rooms offer little more than the basics. It has an indoor pool, gym (with some ageing equipment) and sauna. It's also close to the heart of town and within sight of the pretty Guia Lighthouse. ✎ *Estrada da Vitoria 2–4, Macau • 2855 2222 • www. hotelroyal.com.mo • $$$$*

4 New Century Hotel

Heavy on the marble and chintz, this is unmistakably a gambling hotel. For non-gamblers it's put in the shade somewhat by the lovely Hyatt opposite, but it does offer big rooms and comprehensive guest facilities. ✎ *Av. Padre Tomas Periera 889, Taipa, Macau • 2833 1111 • www.newcentury hotel-macau.com • $$$*

5 Guangdong Victory Hotel

Formerly the Victoria Hotel, this concern occupies two sites on Shamian Island – the main Neo-Classical block and the original colonial building. Facilities include a business centre, a swimming pool and a sauna. ✎ *53 Shamian Bei Jie, Guangzhou • 8121 6688 • www.vhotel.com • $$*

6 Guangdong Hotel, Shenzhen

A reasonably good value option with comfortable, if basic, rooms. Fairly thin on facilities, but with a modest restaurant and smart Japanese-style business centre. ✎ *3033 Shannandong Rd, Shenzhen • 8222 8339 • $$*

7 Century Plaza Hotel

A decent hotel in the heart of Shenzhen with spacious rooms, cable TV, pool, sauna, gym and high-rise karaoke club. ✎ *Kin Chit Rd Shenzhen • 8232 0888 • www. centuryplazahotel-shenzhen. com • $*

8 Crowne Plaza Hotel and Suites Landmark, Shenzhen

This hotel offers luxurious rooms and extensive facilities, including a health club, a driving range, a gym and free Wi-Fi. ✎ *3018 Nanhu Lu, Shenzhen • 8217 2288 • www.ichotelsgroup. com • $$*

9 The Panglin Hotel

Smart and modern, this is one of Shenzhen's superior hotels, about 2 miles (4 km) from the railway station. Room sizes are decent and all come with cable TV. Services include station shuttle bus, babysitting and 24-hour room service. The revolving Skylounge at the top is Shenzhen's highest restaurant. ✎ *2002 Jiabin Lu, Lowu, Shenzhen • 2518 5888 • www. panglin-hotel.com • $$$*

10 Felicity Hotel

This good-value hotel is reasonably well located and even boasts its own art gallery. Standards are high and guests can take advantage of the four restaurants as well as the gym, pool and sauna. ✎ *1085 Heping Lu, Shenzhen • 2558 6333 • www.felicityhotel- shenzhen.com • $$*

For maps of Macau, Shenzhen and Guangzhou **See pp118, 126 & 130**

Nathan Road

Price Categories

For a standard, double room per night (with breakfast if included), taxes and extra charges.		
$	under HK$500
$$	HK$500–$1,000
$$$	HK$1,000–$2,000
$$$$	HK$2,000–$2,500
$$$$$	over HK$2,500

🔟 Value-for-Money Hotels

1 The Salisbury YMCA
Don't be put off by the initials. For value, views and location, the always-popular YMCA, next door to the posh Peninsula, can't be beaten. The well-furnished rooms are spacious, equipped with fax/laptop ports, and satellite and cable TV. A large swimming pool, sauna, gym and indoor climbing wall round off the facili-ties. Family suites have all the basics. A few excellent upmarket dorm beds, too. ◈ *41 Salisbury Rd, Tsim Sha Tsui • Map M4 • 2268 7000 • www. ymcahk.org.hk • $$$*

2 BP International House
The boxy rooms with ugly '80s wallpaper have smallish beds, but the place is clean, efficient and can be cheap, and has lovely views over Kowloon Park. ◈ *8 Austin Rd, Tsim Sha Tsui • Map M2 • 2376 1111 • www.bpih. com.hk • $$$*

3 The Wharney
Right in the increasingly smart centre of Wanchai, the Wharney offers decent surround-ings, a revamped gym and pool, sauna, business centre and a couple of restaurants. Rooms are well appointed but on the small side. ◈ *57–73 Lockhart Road, Wanchai • Map N6 • 2861 1000 • www.wharney.com • $$$*

4 Bishop Lei International House
In a quiet location, close to the park, this hotel's rooms are small for the money, but you pay for proximity to the Escalator. It has an outdoor pool. Long-stay packages are available. ◈ *4 Robinson Rd, Mid-Levels • Map K6 • 2868 0828 • www. bishopleihtl.com.hk • $$$*

5 Garden View International House
Given the location, the prices aren't bad, and even better for long stays (two weeks plus). The decor is 1980s and the rooms smallish. Discounts of 30 to 50 per cent are often available in the low season. ◈ *1 Macdonnell Rd • Map K6 • 2877 3737 • www.ywca.org.hk • $$$*

6 Shamrock
The rather severe lobby opens onto Nathan Road, and the dishevelled lifts lead up to some big rooms with satellite TV, air conditioning and phone. ◈ *23 Nathan Rd • Map N4 • 2735 2271 • www. shamrockhotel.com.hk • $$$*

7 Harbour View International House
This modest Chinese YMCA-run hotel charges a premium for the location, but low-season discounts are available. Baths are pretty small. ◈ *4 Harbour Rd, Wan Chai • Map N5 • 2802 0111 • www.harbourview.com.hk • $$$*

8 2 Macdonnell Road
With pleasant rooms, a good Central location and excellent views across the Zoological and Botan-ical Gardens to the city and harbour, Macdonnell Road offers good value. Rooms have all the basics plus kitchenette. Long-stay packages are also available *(see p153)*. ◈ *2 Macdonnell Rd, Central • Map K6 • 2132 2132 • www.twomr.com.hk • $$$*

9 The Empire Hotel
Marooned between the area's two main roads, the Empire is right in the heart of Wan Chai so you're paying for location rather than luxury, as the cheap fittings will constantly remind you. Still, the prices are competitive, the service isn't bad and there's a small but adequate rooftop pool, plus gym and broadband Internet access. ◈ *33 Hennessey Rd, Wan Chai • Map N6 • 3692 2111 • www. empirehotel.com.hk • $$$*

10 Rosedale on the Park
This self-styled "cyber boutique hotel" offers reasonable value over-looking Victoria Park. The look is sleek and modern, and the small but well laid-out rooms include broadband connection. ◈ *8 Shelter St, Causeway Bay • Map Q6 • 2127 8888 • www.rosedale.com.hk • $$$*

Note: Unless otherwise stated, all hotels accept credit cards, have en-suite bathrooms and air conditioning

Left **Plover Cove** Right **Chungking House**

TOP 10 Cheap Sleeps

1 Anne Black Guest House

If location isn't important then consider the YWCA-run Anne Black Guest House stuck out in Mongkok. The rooms (either with private or communal bathrooms) are basic but clean with air conditioning, TV and telephone. ◎ 5 Man Fuk Rd, Kowloon • Map E4 • 2713 9211 • www.ywca. org.hk • $

2 Booth Lodge

Air-conditioned rooms with shower, bath, fridge, phone and TV are merely adequate but the location and prices are great at this Salvation Army-run hotel. ◎ 11 Wing Sing Lane, Yau Ma Tei, Kowloon • Map N1 • 2771 9266 • www.boothlodge. salvation.org.hk • $$

3 Caritas Bianchi Lodge

Like Booth Lodge next door, there's only a chapel and restaurant-cum-café to amuse yourself here. Still, the rooms are large by any standards. ◎ 4 Cliff Road, Yau Ma Tei, Kowloon • Map N1 • 2388 1111 • www. caritas-chs.org.hk • $$

4 New King's Hotel

Well situated but in something of a chaotic, scrappy and noisy area. Rooms are neat but small, and the views unlovely. ◎ 473 Nathan Rd, Yau Ma Tei, Kowloon • Map N1 • 2780 1281 • $$

5 Holy Carpenter Guest House

A pleasant alternative to the dingier guesthouse offerings in Chungking and Mirador, but stuck out in boring old Hung Hom. Facilities in double and triple rooms are basic but include TV, phone, bathroom, shower and air conditioning. ◎ 1 Dyer Ave, Hung Hom, Kowloon • Map R2 • 2362 0301 • $

6 Bradbury Hall Hostel

As you might expect from its remote location, this hostel has basic, barrack-like dorms. Those with tents may want to walk on and pitch camp at Tai Long Wan's lovely beaches nearby. ◎ Chek Keng, Sai Kung, New Territories • Map F3 • 2328 2458 • www.hihostels.com • $

7 Bradbury Jockey Club Youth Hostel

This very pleasant hostel by the reservoir makes for a good base or stop-off for walkers exploring the beautiful Plover Cove area. Air-conditioned singles, doubles or dorms are available. ◎ 66 Tai Mei Tuk, New Territories • Map F2 • 2662 5123 • www. hihostels.com • $

8 Pak Sha O Hostel

Lying in the heart of the country park, this is a functional hikers' place with dorm beds. The views are great, however, and it's also possible to camp. ◎ Pak Sha O, Hoi Ha Rd, New Territories • Map F2 • 2328 2327 • www.yha.org.hk • $

9 Sze Lok Yuen Hostel

A very basic hikers' crash-pad, Sze Lok Yuen is close to the summit of Tai Mo Shan, Hong Kong's tallest peak. The views are spectacular but its dorm rooms are pretty basic with no fans or air conditioning. The altitude cools things down though in all but the hottest months. Camping is permitted. ◎ Tai Mo Shan, Tseun Wan, New Territories • Map D3 • 2488 8188 • www.yha.org.hk • $

10 Chungking House, Chungking Mansions

Staying at the mansions is a badge of honour to some budget travellers, an unpleasant necessity to others (see p82). The dingy hallways and semi-squalor contain dozens of guesthouses offering cheap and usually stuffy accommodation in an excellent location. Oppressive but fascinating, Chungking Mansions is Hong Kong's cultural melting pot. Chungking House is probably the best option, with larger rooms than elsewhere in Chungking Mansions. ◎ Block 4A/5F, 40 Nathan Rd, Tsim Sha Tsui • Map N4 • 2739 1600 • www.chungkinghouse. com • $

Note: *Unless otherwise stated, all hotels accept credit cards, have en-suite bathrooms and air conditioning*

Price Categories

For a standard, double room per night (with breakfast if included), taxes and extra charges.

$	under HK$500
$$	HK$500–$1,000
$$$	HK$1,000–$2,000
$$$$	HK$2,000–$2,500
$$$$$	over HK$2,500

The Repulse Bay

🔟 Long-Stay Hotels

1 22 Peel St
Centrally located above a bustling produce market, this modern block offers cosy studios and spacious-looking apartments with smart furnishings, daily maid service and, for HK$250 extra, monthly unlimited broadband Internet access. 🌐 22 Peel St, Central • Map K5 • 2522 3082 • www.oakwood.com • HK$32,000–$68,800 per month

2 The Wesley
The fittings are tired and the rooms small, but The Wesley offers very competitive long-stay packages in a central location. Deals include free local calls, maid service, kitchenette, and use of swimming pool and gym at the sister hotel in Quarry Bay. 🌐 22 Hennessey Rd, Wanchai • Map N6 • 2866 6688 • HK$13,800 per month

3 2 Macdonnell Road
Offering smarter and only slightly pricier long-stay accommodation than next door's Garden View. The location is excellent; the views to the harbour and city good. Maid service, free local calls, use of gym, satellite and cable TV, kitchenette and Central shuttle bus are all included in the price. 🌐 2 Macdonnell Rd, Central • Map K6 • 2132 2132 • www.twomr.com.hk • HK$23,000–$60,000 per month

4 Chi Residences
The beautifully appointed rooms here are decorated in a contemporary style. The studios are slightly small but still great value for the location in Central. The larger apartments are highly desirable. 🌐 8/F Wynham Place, 44 Wynham St, Central • Map K5 • 3443 6888 • www.chi-residences.com • HK$16,000–$40,000 per month

5 The Repulse Bay
For executives or small families, these upmarket two-bedroom duplex apartments are a 20-minute ride from Central in serene Repulse Bay. The hole in one of the tower blocks is said to promote good feng shui. 🌐 Repulse Bay • Map E5 • 2292 2879 • www.therepulsebay.com • HK$82,000–$99,000 per month

6 The Bay Bridge
Given the Tseun Wan location, these studio and suite apartments are not for those who must be at the centre of things. The apartments are smart, with kitchenette and shower. 🌐 123 Castle Peak Rd, Yau Kom Tau, Tsuen Wan, Kowloon • Map D3 • 2945 1111 • www.hanglung.com • HK$13,000–$27,000 per month

7 Ovolo Residences
These swanky modern residences are close to the heart of Central. They have all the facilities of a deluxe hotel, including kitchenettes and free Wi-Fi, plus Xbox and Wii gaming. 🌐 222 Hollywood Rd, Sheung Wan • Map J5 • 2165 1000 • www.ovologroup.com • HK$34,000 per month

8 Garden View International House
Very competitive long-stay deals start at two weeks' duration. But decor is tired '80s, and the rooms smallish. Long stayers benefit from maid service, free local calls and Central shuttle bus. 🌐 1 Macdonnell Rd • Map K6 • 2877 3737 www.ywca.org.uk • HK$16,500 per month

9 The Rosedale on the Park
The Rosedale has small, well laid-out rooms with broadband connection and kitchenette. There's also a small gym. 🌐 8 Shelter St, Causeway Bay • Map Q6 • 2127 8888 • www.rosedale.com.hk • HK$22,500–$35,000 per month

10 Yes Inn
Bright, small and inexpensive serviced apartments in a residential area. The cheaper options have TV and Internet, but no kitchenette. 🌐 4/F, 10 Anchor St, Tai Kok Tsui, Kowloon • Map E4 • 3427 6000 • www.yesinn.com • HK$9,000–$19,000 per month

Left **The Warwick** Right **Restaurant, Harbour Plaza Resort City**

🔟 Great Escapes

❶ Hong Kong Gold Coast Hotel

This ten-acre resort offers sea views from its well-equipped rooms. The accommodation complex is unlovely from outside but recreation facilities include pool, pitch-and-putt golf course, tennis courts and running track. 🗺 *No.1 Castle Peak Rd, Kowloon • Map B3 • 2452 8888 • www.sino-hotels.com • $$$*

❷ The Warwick

A cheap alternative to city living, magical Cheung Chau's only major hotel offers fine sea views next to good beaches with windsurf and kayak hire. Great coastal walks are around the headland. Furnishings are nothing special, and the exterior is '60s municipal. 🗺 *East Bay, Cheung Chau • Map C6 • 2981 0081 • $$$*

❸ Harbour Plaza Resort City

Out in the New Territories, this extensive resort complex offers a vast array of sports and recreation facilities, including cinemas, shops, gyms, sports tracks and courts, Chinese and International restaurants, and nearby historical and beauty spots. All rooms include the basics with lounge and kitchenette. 🗺 *18 Tin Yan Rd, Tin Shui Wai, New Territories • Map C2 • 2180 6688 • www.harbour-plaza.com • $$$*

❹ Jockey Club Mount Davis Youth Hostel

An excellent budget option for the adventurous, this lovely and friendly hostel sits atop Mount Butler at the western edge of Hong Kong Island. Take a taxi there. 🗺 *Mount Davis Path, Kennedy Town • Map D5 • 2817 5715 • www.yha.org.uk • $*

❺ Concerto Inn

Hardly a resort hotel but worth a night's escape to leafy, low-rise Lamma Island. Modest but neat air-conditioned rooms with TV and minibar. Lamma's famous Han Lok Yuen pigeon restaurant is nearby *(see p117)*. 🗺 *Hung Shing Ye, Lamma Island • Map D6 • 2982 1668 • www.concertoinn.com.hk • $$*

❻ White Swan Hotel

Overlooking the Pearl River on sleepy Shamian Island, this large but lovely hotel is the place to find peace in Guangzhou. 🗺 *1 Southern St, Shamian Island, Guangzhou • 8188 6968 • www.whiteswanhotel.com • $$$*

❼ Pousada de Sao Tiago

Converted from an old Portuguese fort hewn from the rock in the 17th century, this tiny hotel looking across the bay to mainland China is a picturesque delight. Rooms are heavily but beautifully decorated in Portuguese style. 🗺 *Avenida de Republica, Fortaleza de Sao Tiago de Barra, Macau • 2896 8686 • www.saotiago.com.mo • $$$$$*

❽ Westin Macau

A lovely getaway. All rooms come with their own terrace and sea views. There's a small sandy beach and an 18-hole golf course. You can also practise your swing on the ocean driving range with balls that float. 🗺 *Estrada de Hac Sa 1918, Ilha de Coloane, Macau • 2887 1111 • www.starwoodhotels.com • $$$*

❾ San Va

Step back in time with this genuine 1920s guesthouse. Rooms are unadorned and all facilities are shared. San Va is clean, romantic and lovingly run. 🗺 *65–67 Rua da Felicidade, Macau • www.sanvahotel.com • No credit cards • $*

❿ Pousada de Coloane

This tiny, remote hotel lies at the far end of Coloane overlooking a small, pretty beach. It boasts a nice deck area, swimming pool, and attractive Portuguese-style restaurant and bar. Room fittings show their age, but at least they are well equipped. 🗺 *Praia Chok Van, Coloane Island, Macau • 2888 2143 • www.hotelpocoloane.com.mo • $$*

Note: *Unless otherwise stated, all hotels accept credit cards, have en-suite bathrooms and air conditioning*

General Index